# Graying
## Gracefully

# Graying

## Gracefully

## Preaching to Older Adults

William J. Carl, Jr.

*editor*

Westminster John Knox Press
Louisville, Kentucky

Scripture quotations from the New Revised Standard Version
of the Bible are copyright © 1989 by the Division of Christian Education
of the National Council of the Churches of Christ in the U.S.A.
and are used by permission.

Acknowledgments will be found on page xi.

*Book design by Jennifer K. Cox*
*Cover design by Alec Bartsch*
*Cover photograph courtesy of Publishers Depot*™

*First edition*
Published by Westminster John Knox Press
Louisville, Kentucky

This book is printed on acid-free paper that meets the
American National Standards Institute Z39.48 standard. ∞

PRINTED IN THE UNITED STATES OF AMERICA
97 98 99 00 01 02 03 04 05 06 — 10 9 8 7 6 5 4 3 2 1

**Library of Congress Cataloging-in-Publication Data**

Graying gracefully : preaching to older adults / William J.
  Carl, Jr., editor. — 1st ed.
      p.    cm.
  Includes bibliographical references.
  ISBN 0-664-25722-4 (alk. paper)
    1. Preaching to the aged.   2. Aged—Religious life.   3. Church
work with the aged.   4. Sermons, American.   5. Aging—Religious
aspects—Christianity—Sermons.   I. Carl, William J., 1923-
BV4235.A44G73   1997
252'.56—dc20                     96-43254

*To God's Glory*
*In Memory Of*
*William J. and Evelyn B. Carl*
*Who Grew Old Gracefully*
*To God's Glory*

# Contents

# Preface

The idea for a book on preaching to older adults began with a concern for their increasing numbers in the general population and among worshiping congregations. It matters not whether you talk about the local congregation or the hairline of worshipers—the temple is graying and has been for some time. Following a discussion of preaching and older adults with President William Tabbernee of Phillips Theological Seminary, the theme "the gospel and the graying temple" was approved for the Oreon E. Scott Lectures at the University of Tulsa campus. All the contributors to this edited volume participated in the Scott Lectures, with the exception of Father Walter J. Burghardt, S.J., who graciously agreed to contribute a chapter on the contemplation of what is truly meaningful, especially in the later years of life.

One may ask: Why a lecture series and a subsequent book on the subject of preaching to older adults? A survey of literature on older adults indicated that sociologists, psychologists, politicians, and financial advisors had all studied and written on various factors regarding persons fifty-five years of age or older. Those who have addressed the various religious aspects of this older-age set of society have for the most part dealt only with biblical views, pastoral care, and church programming. The specific issue of preaching to older adults remained largely unaddressed.

During my seminary days I learned that Robert Worth Frank, president of McCormick Theological Seminary, considered everything philosophically. Years later at the age of eighty-five, in an unpublished collection of talks on aging, he commented in his typical reflective style on all the how-to books, saying, "There is no book on 'how to grow old,' either gracefully or disgracefully." This collection of chapters and sermons is a homiletical attempt to fill that gap by helping preachers help others discover for themselves how to grow old gracefully to God's glory.

This is a book about understanding and preaching to those who want to grow old gracefully and to those who are striving to grow old grace-fully. Its intent is to provide practical information, as well as biblical and theological insights, to older adults and to those who preach to older adults; to help all its readers relate biblical and theological insights to the experience of growing older; and to provide a focus for those who preach to older adults in terms of their current needs on a biblical and theological basis relative to a holistic life experience. It also seeks to disclose the insensitive bias from which many who preach God's word speak in relation to older adults—their perspective, needs, and concerns. Preachers who lack an intentional sensitivity for older adults unthinkingly speak in a way that I hope is disappearing, one that must end if preaching is ever to be truly meaningful to older adults, at least in a caring pastoral sense.

This book in no sense pretends to be the final word on preaching and older adults; at best, it is an initial word. It looks at some of the biblical and spiritual aspects, as well as some of the pastoral concerns, of how to preach to and about older adults, their needs, and their concerns. It does not primarily consider the church's historical experience with or perspective toward older adults, nor does its limited scope permit an extensive survey of the changing views of various theologies toward older adults, though such aspects are considered variously throughout it. Such historical and theological topics and other appropriate issues remain for another time and perhaps for others to pursue in greater depth.

I acknowledge my appreciation to all my colleagues and students at Phillips Theological Seminary who have so willingly reflected with me on the place and purpose of preaching to older adults. I am also grateful to all those dear souls who have patiently borne with my sometimes feeble, fumbling attempts to preach to them as older adults with a plethora of varied needs—those who made me realize a book on preaching to older adults needed to be written. I thank each of the contributors to this volume, and especially Timothy G. Staveteig of Westminster John Knox Press, for putting up with my prodding, plodding style of coordinating this venture.

Most particularly, I acknowledge my great debt of gratitude to my mother and father, who first nurtured me in the faith and then witnessed to how their trust in God enabled them to pass gracefully through the various stages of life into old age as they both lived and died to God's glory.

I also thank my wife, who is always forbearing, supportive, and patient with me in all my labors for the Lord. At one point, however, she did express an older adult concern when she sweetly but firmly said, "Finish that book so you can help take care of the grandchildren when they come." And believe me, I got busy because I knew I had more than one reason to be—even though I am getting older—there are those who still need me, both young and old. So I acknowledge my appreciation to my wife and all the rest of my family who have offered helpful suggestions and meaningful insights, but most of all to God to whose glory I pray always to live and gray gracefully.

William J. Carl, Jr.
Easter 1996

# Acknowledgments

Grateful acknowledgment is made to the following for permission to reproduce copyrighted material:

Christian Century Foundation, from "What Shall I Do with My Life?" by Howard Thurman, copyright 1939 Christian Century Foundation. Reprinted by permission from the September 1939 issue of *The Christian Pulpit*.

GIA Publications, Inc., from "God It Was," in *Iona Community: Love from Below*, copyright G. I. A. Publications, Inc.

Harcourt Brace & Company, excerpts from "Confession Overheard in a Subway," in *Afternoon of a Pawnbroker and Other Poems*, by Kenneth Fearing, copyright 1943 by Kenneth Fearing and renewed 1971 by Bruce Fearing; reprinted by permission of Harcourt Brace & Company.

New Directions Publishing Corp., from "Do Not Go Gentle into That Good Night," by Dylan Thomas, in *The Poems of Dylan Thomas*, copyright © 1952 by Dylan Thomas. Reprinted by permission of New Directions Publishing Corp.

New Directions Publishing Corp., from "Evening Train," by Denise Levertov, in *Evening Train*, copyright © 1992 by Denise Levertov. Reprinted by permission of New Directions Publishing Corp.

Society of Jesus, New York Province, for sermon "Aging, Changing, Giving," from Walter J. Burghardt, S.J., *Speak the Word with Boldness*, Paulist Press, 1994.

# Contributors

### Jon L. Berquist

A minister in the Christian Church (Disciples of Christ) and an editor for Westminster John Knox Press; author of articles, papers, and books, including *Ancient Wine, New Wineskins: The Lord's Supper in Old Testament Perspective; Reclaiming Her Story: The Witness of Women in the Old Testament; Ezekiel: Surprises by the River;* and *Judaism in Persia's Shadow: A Social and Historical Approach.*

### Walter J. Burghardt, S.J.

Senior Fellow at the Woodstock Theological Center and founder of Woodstock's national project, "Preaching the Just Word"; a priest and member of the Society of Jesus in the Roman Catholic Church; teacher, lecturer, writer, and preacher; editor of *The Living Pulpit;* and author of numerous articles and fifteen books, including *Sir, We Would Like to See Jesus* and *Still Proclaiming Your Wonders.*

### David G. Buttrick

Professor of Homiletics and Liturgics at the Divinity School of Vanderbilt University, Nashville, Tennessee; a United Church of Christ minister and popular preacher; lecturer at more than fifty colleges and universities, including Harvard, Yale, and the University of Chicago; author of numerous articles and ten books, including *Homiletic, Preaching Jesus Christ, The Mystery and the Passion,* and *A Captive Voice: The Liberation of Preaching.*

### Cynthia M. Campbell

President of McCormick Theological Seminary, Chicago, Illinois; formerly Pastor of First Presbyterian Church, Salina, Kansas; lecturer; author of *Feminist Theology: An Introductory Study* and coauthor of *We Decide Together.*

### William J. Carl, Jr.

Professor of Preaching and Reformed Studies at Phillips Theological Seminary (University of Tulsa campus), and Pastor Emeritus of the Good Shepherd Presbyterian Church of Bartlesville, Oklahoma; has served as industrial evangelist in a mission to the Philippines, and as adjunct professor of psychology and psychotherapist on a psychiatric staff; author of a number of articles on preaching, including "Politics and Preaching?" and "Stewards of Suffering."

### William J. Carl III

Pastor of the First Presbyterian Church of Dallas, Texas; formerly Associate Professor of Homiletics and Worship and Instructor of New Testament Greek at Union Theological Seminary at Richmond, Virginia; sermon editor for *Homiletic*; and author of a number of articles and books, including *Preaching Christian Doctrine, Church People Beware!* and *Waiting for the Lord.*

### Joseph R. Jeter, Jr.

Granville and Erline Walker Associate Professor of Homiletics at the Brite Divinity School of Texas Christian University, Fort Worth, Texas; a Christian Church (Disciples of Christ) minister; lecturer and author of numerous articles and books, including *Fruit of the Spirit: The "Triple Trinity" of Galatians 5, Alexander Procter: The Sage of Independence,* and *Thirteen Sermons from the National Radio Pulpit.*

### James Earl Massey

Dean Emeritus of Anderson University School of Theology, Anderson, Indiana; a Church of God minister, he has served as pastor in Detroit, Michigan, missionary in Jamaica, West Indies, and preacher for five years on an international radio ministry that reached throughout the English-speaking world; lecturer and author of numerous articles and eighteen books, including *Designing the Sermon, The Sermon in Perspective,* and *The Responsible Pulpit.*

# 1

## The Graying Temple Is Here and Now: A Challenge to Preaching

*William J. Carl, Jr.*

While there is an ever-increasing older adult population, many pastors have not yet reached that age themselves. Ross Henry Larson, a Lutheran consultant on Ministries in Aging with Generage, reports that younger ministers tell him "they feel patronized by older persons who treat them as youth rather than pastors." He says younger ministers "imagine themselves to be poor advisers to persons who play the role of parents or even grandparents."[1] What's more, younger ministers have not lived through those dynamic experiences that their older church members know so well—the Great Depression, World War II, the Korean Conflict, and in some cases, not even the turbulent 1960s and the Vietnam War. Hence such major events are only occasionally recognized and seldom included in even a sermon illustration by young preachers, who often misunderstand or misappropriate these events in terms of the formational foundations they pose for the fears, frustrations, hopes, and aspirations of older adults.[2] On the other hand, older ministers need to guard against preaching so much from their own age perspective that they fail to proclaim biblical and theological solutions to problems rather than their own age-dominated opinions.

Since older adult church members are a disproportionately large percentage of participants and worshipers at the close of the twentieth century, preaching provides a good vehicle for addressing their needs.[3] Generalized results from 1992 congregational surveys confirmed the need for an informed homiletic in terms of preaching to older adults.[4] One student, commenting on the small rural community in which his parish was located, wrote, "The majority of all residents are over sixty-five, although very few are actually retired." Another student, serving as an associate pastor in a multiple-staff church in a metropolitan center, wrote, "The congregation is 64 percent female and 36 percent male. The average age is 59 years old. Sixty percent of the membership is over 60 years of age." Another student reported that his congregation designated a survey category titled "Funding/

Providing Aging Parent Care" as one of three basic concerns and a category titled "Finding Retirement Opportunities" as one of the respondents' four "hopes and dreams."

Preaching provides a good way to inform others concerning the needs and care of older adults, as well as to become a voice of advocacy in their behalf. Divine justice for the elderly is clearly stated in the law (Ex. 22:22–26; 23:9–11) and for those who are in need also in the Holiness Code (Lev. 19:9–13).[5] Those who preach to older adults need also to speak out in their behalf. Barbara Nilsen rightly maintains, "It is not enough to be present to those who suffer and console them; we must expose suffering caused by injustice and struggle against it even if it means that we put ourselves at risk." She goes on to say, "We also must be prepared to hear the voice of judgment and willingly give up privileges we have gained at the expense of others."[6] A minister's uninformed perspective, attitude, knowledge, experience, and/or lack of insight in these critical areas of pastoral ministry with older adults may unknowingly contribute to fostering a prejudicial view of aging, both in the church and the community.

A good insight into preaching to older adults is not only a present need but will be a continuing need. A Merrill Lynch Baby Boomer Retirement Index, based on a nationwide survey of more than two thousand households, estimated that 76 million Americans aged thirty-five to forty-eight will reach older adulthood early in the twenty-first century.[7] An Alliance for Aging Research survey found that "two-thirds of Americans want to live to age 100, 69% believe they'll live beyond the current average life expectancy of 75 years," and "75% fear losing their physical independence as they grow older."[8] Obviously, understanding the needs of older adults, as well as understanding how both the Hebrew and Christian scriptures speak to older adults and to others in their behalf, is not only a present concern but a future need.

## Understanding Older Adults

The first step in understanding older adults is getting in touch with what they think and feel. That means, in part, asking them. When asked what to preach to older adults, one very knowledgable lay leader observed: "Don't presume they know what they need to know about the Christian faith—preach doctrine. They have life crisis needs without the spiritual basis and/or reserves to meet those needs. Provide for their needs before they die." In light of the present and looking to the future, Leith Anderson suggests the following:

> The primary content of sermons for the 21st century should be the Word of God. This is theologically necessary because the Bible

represents God's communication to humans and the source of our information on salvation and life. To omit the Bible or merely use the Bible as a "jumping-off spot" for the preacher's opinion is presumptuous. It assumes that what we have to say is more important than what God has to say. Indeed, on a practical level people are weary of the bombardment of human opinions. Modern Americans feel so attacked by multiple messages that they are not likely to come to the church for one more. They want an authoritative message from God that is distinctively different from all the others. They come to hear what God has to say.[9]

Most older adults would agree. Generally they tend to be serious-minded folk at a serious-minded time of life who are interested in a religious point of view.[10]

Older adults, however, often have a limited personal perspective. The following observations were made by a group of older adults in a retirement center, who were asked how and what ministers should preach in terms of older adults: "We don't want to hear more about aging; we're more interested in considering how today's social, economic, and political ills will impact our grandchildren." Others observed: "Don't tell us what not to do." "Don't give us another book review." "Help us handle the fact that we're on the downhill side, that we're no longer what we used to be." "Give us something happy; we have enough of the downside of life." "What is life eternal, heaven, and the afterlife really like?" Asking most older adults what to preach or what they need or want to get from preaching, however, seldom brings meaningful answers. For the most part, they have neither a knowledge of homiletics nor a broad-spectrum grasp of scripture, nor, for that matter, of the human situation other than their own personal one and their present circumstances.

## Homiletical Concerns
## for Older Adults

Both the hope and promise of the gospel need to be proclaimed to all ages since the process of aging is a constant reminder of human frailty. Even the best medical care money can buy does not forestall the inevitability of human mortality. The intentional preaching of the gospel to the needs of all ages, but most especially to those of older adults, is a challenging task. The gospel is the gospel to whomever it is preached, but there are ways of communicating the gospel to different age-sets, as well as to different circumstances, that do determine how well the word of God is received and appropriated.

There is no intent to imply that there is some kind of special geriatric theology or, for that matter, a geriatric homiletic. Quite the contrary, older persons need to be mainstreamed in both the church and the community as much as is possible. Francis Park, pastor of the Faith Presbyterian Church in Sun City, Arizona, holds that older persons need to know there is life after retirement; they need to experience a sense of joy and forgiveness, a sense of justice, without feeling God is a cosmic policeman; they need to know the unconditional love of God. He feels that all too many older adults have an inaccurate childhood concept of what preaching is. He proposes an expository style of biblical preaching that relates our story to the biblical story. He also feels that preaching geared to older-adult needs can help others deal with these same problems when they become older adults.[11]

In a sense, preaching is preaching, to whomever it is directed, so why consider preaching to older adults to be different? The choice of scriptures, texts, themes, and subjects may seem to be little different for any age-set if preachers are true to the gospel message. Yet the way in which older adults perceive and appropriate that which is preached may be different, depending on the intensity of their concern, their present needs, and the issues being considered.

Older adults confront all the cultural changes and personal difficulties that confront everyone in our society, as well as the personal changes that come with later life.[12] This ever-increasing confluence of personal and social changes challenges their ever-diminishing available strength. Likewise, every preacher of God's word is challenged to proclaim the counseling comfort of God's word to a growing number of older adults in both the church and the community.[13]

Human experience during the advancing years in life takes on a new sense of urgency based on the limited time one has left to live, as well as one's present circumstances. In any case, a sermon preached with older adults in mind is something more than a counterpart for or obverse side of a children's sermon. Sermons addressed to older adults need to minister to the brokenness of the human condition during the later years of life, as well as to nurture the wholeness of life.

Older adults gradually move from an upward-and-onward stance to a settling-down phase and ultimately to their final phaseout. Even without universal coverage, an improved and more widely available medical care system is increasing the life span in America. With more years to live, better health, and earlier retirement, many older adults see no relationship between their faith experience and how they will live during this sometimes insecure later phase of life.[14]

Some see old age as something to avoid, as if that were possible—as a marginally acceptable alternative to dying. Joan Rachel Goldberg maintains that "marriage and family therapists (MFTs), like non-mental health professionals, have slighted what lies beyond the middle years."[15] William Auld notes that "religion and gerontology have traveled separate paths": a better job is done with the earlier phases of life, such as baptism, confirmation, and marriage, than is done with the later phases, such as grand-parenting, retirement, and death.[16] The first is not to be slighted, and the last is not to be ignored.

God moves mightily even during old age, as the biblical record confirms again and again, granting wisdom and other blessings to those who are old (Job 12:12). Consider the children born late in life to Abraham and Sarah (Gen. 21:2) and to Zechariah and Elizabeth (Luke 1:18, 36). And there is Isaiah, who proclaimed not only a divine creation but a carrying of God's people even into old age (Isa. 46:4).

While research on aging and the elderly has increased, the study of how and what to preach to this ever-increasing new frontier of society has for the most part been ignored. Preaching the gospel to graying temples at the turn of the century demands attention. And it will be an exciting challenge preachers will continue to face as each year more Baby Boomers approach age fifty-five. Craig Miller observes:

> America is undergoing its own revolution. While its ideals of democracy and freedom are breaking out across the globe, American society is moving into a new era. This American revolution is based on the slow turn of demographic forces that is transferring power and leadership to the Baby Boomer generation. This generation of 77 million Americans—almost one-third of the population of the United States—was born during the postwar economic boom from 1946 to 1964, and will be ages thirty-six to fifty-four in the year 2000. As we move through the 1990s and head into a new millennium, the Baby Boomer generation will set the agenda for the United States and, thus, for a world that looks to North America for its vision of the future.[17]

Change is definitely in the making and the preaching of the gospel to a graying temple demands new ways of proclaiming old truths.

## Preaching to Those Who Will Hear

When Joel issued his prophetic call for prayerful repentance, he called for the sanctifying of the congregation of God's people. The children were to be brought together and the aged assembled (1:13–2:17). One can only speculate on why Joel singled out the young and the old. Perhaps it was the innocence of children and the faithfulness of the aged or that older adults had already tried everything else and knew their hope and that of the nation was in God alone. After all, Joel's prophecy is addressed to the fickle faith of the masses who buy into every secular, materialistic idolatry imaginable.

Preachers who seek a repentant revival of faith do well to heed Joel's practice of starting with those who are most likely to respond—the young and the old. Based on a 1991 survey, George Barna reported that 58 percent of older adults (fifty-five years old or older) and 46 percent of younger adults (eighteen to twenty-five years old) rated preaching at their church as "excellent" while only 39 percent of those twenty-six to fifty-four years old felt that way.[18] Older adults may be the most likely group in the church to help increase a sense of faith and faithfulness among God's people and throughout the community.

Renewal demands a starting point. When the priests and ministers of the Lord wept and prayed for God's mercy and help, God gave an immediate response (Joel 2:17–19). Preachers who seek a sense of renewal among God's people need to proclaim that wonderful day of the Lord, when the Holy Spirit will pour forth and even those who are older will dream again (Joel 2:28) of all that is good and is possible when the blessings of God flow forth.

In a throwaway age most products and appliances have built-in obsolescence, which is hard for older adults to understand—especially those who grew up during the Great Depression, when they had to make everything last as long as they could. Things that had been around a long time were not only good but treasured, such as works of art, a Stradivarius violin, or old gold that always has an intrinsic value and is never outdated. Then came the silicon society with its software programs that were passé before they were installed on computer hardware that had just been bought and was already outdated. Finally, recycling of waste products became a necessity, with that which had served one purpose being used again for another. Why not human beings? Was Jesus wrong? Are not human beings of more value than material things? A growing number of older adults believe they are of more value and are retraining themselves to begin second and sometimes third careers.

Loren Dutton, in his book *The Vintage Years*, reports from numerous interviews that "the five things that most often get in the way of greater happiness for older people are concerns about their health, financial worries, sexual frustration, family problems and apprehension about the future."[19] He concludes there is no simple formula for happiness in the later years in life, any more than there is in any other time in life. He, however, suggests that all of us must accept responsibility for our own welfare and that we all need to be reminded that the time to be happy is the present and the place is where we are. Preaching to an older constituency needs to inspire this kind of attitude.

Kenneth Stokes, in an article titled "A Growing Faith after 60," outlined four faith tasks of older adulthood—adjusting to retirement and loss of power, keeping mentally and spiritually alert, adjusting to changing cultural values and patterns, and personal preparation for death.[20] What is most important both for older adults as the recipients of preaching as well as for those who preach to them is not so much this agenda of needs but the fact that older adults are still capable of growth and development, personally and spiritually. Growth and development during the later years of life will be discussed further in chapter 8.

Preaching to older adults involves all the personal concerns as well as the social and spiritual issues that need attention in any other stage of life plus some special concerns. Older people, however, tend to encounter the things that are common to everyone else more often than others do. They are also less likely to recover from or outlive these experiences as easily or as quickly as a younger person will. These common needs and problems also occur in combination and with greater frequency among those who are older than they do with those who are younger, making them more difficult to endure and/or handle, such as illness, death of family and friends, and loneliness. In view of this more frequent occurrence of difficulties and a loss of resiliency to bounce back, the older person often finds it harder to feel hopeful about the future.

## Sensitivity toward Others

In spite of whatever insight preachers may have in terms of the issues, themes, and topics involved in preaching the gospel to a graying temple, some may also need a course in sensitivity training. A newspaper reporter, in a report on a sensitivity training program for health workers, wrote that an "aging person can face the loss of sight, hearing, mobility or physical power, but the loss of dignity may be the most painful." Wallace told how a thirty-eight-year-old nurse in a sensitivity training program had to role-play a seventy-five-year-old retired person who was a patient in a hospital setting. In her role, the nurse sat tied in a wheelchair as people stood beside her and ignored her. They talked about her without consulting her. They made decisions about her without even glancing toward her. Nobody listened to her or even gave her eye contact. She said, "I didn't realize how degrading some things can be."[21]

The first step in terms of sensitivity is illustrated by the cartoon in which an older man is sitting across the desk from an agency person who asks him, "Do you prefer to be called 'Geriatric,' 'Elderly' or 'Senior'?" With a heavy frown, the man responds, "I prefer to be called Mr. Stevens." That, of course, is a reminder to all who preach that negative, pejorative, put-down, patronizing, exclusive language is always out of place in the pulpit. At all times and in all places (especially in the pulpit) such demeaning references and patronizing terms as "Sweetie," "Honey," "Dear," "Pop," or "Gramps" are inappropriate. Few if any older adults want to be thought of as the "chronologically gifted," a "goldie oldie," "superannuated," "old geezer," "old biddy" or "old fogey," a "Medicare Christian," "shut-in," or even a "senior citizen."[22]

In a TV interview, the editor of *Roget's Thesaurus* said he didn't get *Wrinkly* and *Wrinklesville* as synonyms for older folk and retirement communities in his latest edition though he thought he should have. It all seemed humorous to him. He showed no inkling that no more ways are needed to imply undesirable obsolescence for an ever-increasing component of our society, one to which everyone who lives long enough will eventually belong. Add to that the term "granny-dumping," for deserting an elderly person at a hospital emergency room door or elsewhere and you begin to realize how careful we need to be in selecting the terminology we use in referring to this sensitive segment of our society. Does not the Fifth Commandment at least imply simple respect, particularly for parents (Ex. 20:12), as well as for all elderly persons (2 Kings 2:23–24)?

Most preachers do not think of themselves as insensitive, but all too many are when it comes to preaching in nursing-home situations. Few are skilled in such preaching. The most significant barriers for the aged are not the physical stairs and bathrooms that still need to be made barrier-free (as important as they are), but rather the spiritual, social, and emotional barriers created by a personal lack of understanding. Those who preach to older adults need to know that the threshold of understanding is to understand that no one can truly understand how someone else may feel.[23] This lack of insight into how others feel may be the reason preachers often proclaim what older adults perceive to be chidings, not good tidings. Sermons to older adults are preferably proclamations of promise, not pronouncements of punishment.

## A Homiletic of
## Do's and Don'ts

In communicating the gospel to a graying temple, preachers need to be concerned about the terminology they use, their use of scripture, their illustrations, their topics, and their styles of preaching, as well as the interfacing and integration of the other liturgical aspects of worship. They need to preach the gospel to older adults with all the best homiletical skills used on any other occasion so the mind can be taught, the heart touched, and the will moved. The same litany of ills that is to be avoided in preaching in general also needs to be avoided in preaching to older adults. They include, but are not limited to, the following:

> Using too many platitudes
>
> Being too tentative in appeal and approach
>
> Not being sufficiently current
>
> Sounding out of touch with personal and social needs
>
> Showing lack of depth, substance, and theology
>
> Giving a poor delivery
>
> Showing no sense of excitement or charisma
>
> Revealing inadequate preparation
>
> Delivering half-baked messages (Hos. 7:8)

Older adults not only deserve good preaching, they have generally read and studied the scriptures more than younger generations and in turn expect more biblical references and theological substance from those who preach than do most who are younger.

Presidents from Kennedy to Clinton have used the springboard of a few words in the native tongue of those to whom they were speaking in order to establish rapport with them. In like manner preachers do well to season what they preach with bits of the vernacular familiar to their hearers to get and keep their attention and appropriation of what is being preached.

All preachers have language barriers to overcome or work around. As has already been noted, every year more and more preachers know less and less personally about the Great Depression, World War II, and even the turbulent 1960s and the Vietnam War, yet they preach to older adults who do. Obviously this creates a language barrier in terms of clichés, slang, and even the everyday prevailing vernacular, to say nothing about the character and type of illustrations used. The preacher who speaks out of only one time period is definitely handicapped. An older adult church member told an older minister finishing an interim pastorate just before a much younger pastor was to be installed, "My husband and I hate to see you go; you speak our language." Obviously younger preachers, older preachers, and all those in between need a vocabulary that spans a broad spectrum of ages and experiences to preach to people representing a broad spectrum of ages and experiences—especially those of the older and younger generations. Such a vocabulary can be developed through conversations with persons of various ages, pastoral visitation, and some study of modern history.

Preachers need to do all they can to see that language doesn't become a barrier in preaching to all God's people. Admittedly most of the population in general and, some would say, even most church members are biblically illiterate. Hence the answer lies not only in bridging the language gap but in educating both people and preacher so meaningful communication can take place. How else can the intergenerational exchange that is so desperately needed not only in the church but among family members and in the community come about?

The whole task of preaching to older persons, of necessity, involves the preacher's attitude toward older persons in general. If our preaching begins with a patronizing attitude in sermon preparation and ends with a patronizing attitude in delivery, however subtle our attitude may be, it will be perceived by the older adult and our preaching will be discounted in part or disregarded entirely. If, however, our attitude is appreciatively positive, our preaching will be received that way.

## Demythologizing Old Age

The first step to a right attitude toward older persons is to get rid of all the myths about old age. A *Reader's Digest* article listed myths about old age; knowing the facts and discounting these myths, it said, "can make the later years a happier time for those we love and enable us to anticipate growing older without anxiety." The myths are: Anyone older than sixty-four is over the hill; and most older people are poor, lose their sex drive, are usually sick, become senile, and wind up in nursing homes. The concluding words provide a provocative thought for everyone who preaches to older adults: "Once we have freed ourselves of unfounded, counterproductive, even health-threatening myths about old age, we can help the elderly—and ourselves—to live creatively and richly and to stay actively involved throughout life."[23] Even though these myths are often logically denied, they are also often unconsciously embraced. They must be exposed and debunked as misconceptions and half-truths to engender a more positive attitude toward older persons and the aging process.

Unfortunately, in our society old age is usually portrayed in dismal, debilitating, depressing ways that are largely untrue. Gail Sheehy reports on her experience in attending a conference called "The New Older Woman." From this gathering of a diverse group of older women, she says, "A common denominator emerged: The source of continuing aliveness was to find your passion and pursue it with whole heart and single mind." She also noted that "children who grow up with stereotypical views" of older persons are later on "unable to relate to people who don't fit their preconceptions." Sheehy also reports that a psychological study of persons who have achieved active and creative "Second Adulthoods" well into old age revealed that they are more concerned "with feeding the soul than the ego."[24] G. H. Asquith Jr. proposes that pastors need to help older persons confront the physical, financial, social, and vocational limitations of older age with a sense of faith values that will transcend their present limits.[25] Preaching to older adults, as well as to all the rest who are hopefully on their way to becoming older adults, needs to refute the misleading myths about older persons in general with the positive affirmations of God's word.

The last verse of the last chapter of the Hebrew scriptures says that the promised return of the prophet Elijah will usher in a new understanding between the older and younger generations. In fact, Elijah is not only to turn the hearts of parents to their children, he is to turn the hearts of the younger generation to an appreciative understanding of the older generation. This book is primarily concerned with relating those who preach to those who hear—especially to those of an older generation who share with us a graying temple.

## A Preview of What's to Come

In chapter 2, Walter J. Burghardt, S.J., presents an inspirational view of true reality that anyone may embrace at any stage in life and that is especially worthwhile in the later years of life. As a skilled preacher, he invites people and preacher alike to gaze beyond the surface of the material to the substance of the spiritual in a long loving look at true reality in holy living and holy dying. As one of many years, who practices what he preaches, Father Burghardt offers to both older adults and those who preach to them five aspects in the contemplation of God's gifts in life that are so often overlooked or taken for granted and little appreciated.

In chapter 3, David Buttrick addresses a biblical view of the dialectic of age as well as what the Bible says about aging in terms of both the young and the old. He acknowledges that the Bible is both bluntly realistic and yet positive about the Golden Age. It is realistic—"three score and ten" and, if more, then "trouble." He also recognizes the biblical concepts in terms of the pleasures of an extended old age, not the least of which are earthy pleasures. He shows how the Bible speaks of all these things as well as senility at the same time it speaks of wisdom.

In chapter 4, Jon L. Berquist examines sociological factors of aging during the time of both the Old Testament and the New Testament. He considers the issues of life span and age expectations, as well as the changing roles throughout aging and the attitudes of others toward the elderly. Examples from the Pentateuch and from the legal codes illustrate these social patterns and perspectives. He notes that deuterocanonical or apocryphal writings manifest a more moderate approach than do the Hebrew scriptures. He recognizes the brevity of the life span during the period of the early church and that in a sense first-century Christianity was a rebel movement that of necessity had to reject the older ways of faith and life. He also offers five texts that provide specific insights for preaching the gospel to a graying temple. He concludes by

considering the breath of God in terms of human mortality and the experience of death.

In chapter 5, Cynthia Campbell reflects on the loss/grief factor as it significantly affects those who are growing older and feel all their family and
friends are gone or dying. She looks at such themes for preaching to older
adults as where to look for God's presence, letting go of the past, and discovering the comfort and strength that comes from knowing God cares.
She also considers the place of the funeral and memorial service in ministering to older adults. Basically, she proposes that preaching to older adults
should help them make sense of the changes God is bringing in their lives.

In chapter 6, Joseph Jeter considers the place of memory relative to older
adults. Professor Jeter proposes that worship is an act of memory and therefore especially important to those who are older. Preaching to older adults
should hold hope and memory in tension, he suggests, and the stories of the
elderly must not be overlooked in the preaching process. He feels many
adults are just waiting to realize the hope they first found in Christ.

In chapter 7, James Earl Massey considers the biblical view of aging with
the use of genealogies, Genesis, Psalms, and Ecclesiastes. In terms of a
prophetic word for today, Dr. Massey holds that the church needs to be an
advocate for the aging. He considers the disjunction of the family and its impact on the aging, the place of loneliness and the loss of friendships, and the
loss of familiar values in terms of a changing morality. He recommends a style
of preaching that is comforting and serves as a catalyst for remembering.

In chapter 8, I address an agenda for preaching with a catalogue of concerns that are particularly pertinent to older adults. Someone has said that
preachers spend their time answering questions that nobody's asking.
Sometimes the questions nobody seems to be asking are the very questions
that need answers because they compose that hidden agenda that underlies
the most basic of human needs. This chapter looks at a number of these
concerns in terms of preaching to older adults.

Each chapter is followed by a sermon that has been preached sometime,
somewhere by the author of the previous essay. The only exception is the
sermon in chapter 1, "What's So Good about Getting Old?" which was
preached by the editor's son, William J. Carl III—pastor of the First Presbyterian Church of Dallas, Texas.

I hope this book will provoke other reflective studies in terms of preaching the gospel to a graying temple; that it will help to generate a greater
sensitivity to the needs and issues facing older adults; and that it will provide some new insights into how the scriptures speak to the needs of
everyone in the aging process of life. Likewise, I hope that throughout the
pages that follow preachers will find some grist for their sermonic mill
that can be ground, refined, and used to feed the spiritual needs of others,
especially those of an older generation. Last, I hope these chapters will

not only challenge those who preach God's word to be mindful of all ages and classes of hearers but will enable them to preach with greater confidence—especially to those with graying hair.

Peter, preaching at Pentecost, quoted the prophet Joel, who declared that in the last days the young will see visions and the old will dream dreams (Acts 2:17). It is true that older folk may not be as visionary as they were when they were young, but they still have aspirations to pursue and dreams that can come true. The preaching of the gospel to a graying temple needs to excite that possibility and reinforce that reality.

### SERMON

## What's So Good about Getting Old?

### William J. Carl III

*Occasion for sermon:* In the relentless regularity of Sunday morning, the lectionary usually dictates the direction preachers will take in the pulpit. Such was the case when I looked at the appointed passages for June 5, 1994—1 Sam. 8:1–6 and 2 Cor. 4:16–5:1—and began to work on the sermon for the week. I added Ps. 71:9, 18; Ps. 92:12–15; and Heb. 11:11–12 on my own, as it is sometimes my practice to do.

Part of the reason for tilting toward a gerontological theme was that there are many older adults at First Presbyterian Church in Dallas, Texas, where I was pastor at the time, and I felt that these texts spoke specifically to them. The other reason was that my own father, William J. Carl, Jr., the editor of this book, had just celebrated a birthday, was growing older, and was facing a debilitating cancer without a lot of hope. Being a child of the Great Depression, he was not ready to quit working or living and was not at all ready to "go gentle into that good night."

As an unabashed Baby Boomer from a generation that is just now beginning to think seriously about retirement and the end of life, I decided to try in this sermon to hear what these texts might be saying to my people, my father, and me. The sermon "What's So Good about Getting Old?" was the result of that homiletical effort. I am pleased to report that, through a miraculous recovery by the grace and providence of God and the power of prayer and chemotherapy, Dad is able to experience it all firsthand and to finish this book as a gift to many who need to hear also and who need to be heard. To God be the glory.

What's so good about getting old? is a question we all ask. But the way we ask it is a matter of perspective, isn't it? Grade-schoolers ask it with twenty somethings in mind. In the 1960s we Baby Boomers asked it because we didn't trust anybody over thirty; now we think forty or fifty sounds young.

Perhaps age really is a state of mind. But not to those who are getting closer and closer to meeting their Maker. For them the question becomes more poignant each day. What's so good about getting old? What indeed?

At his eightieth birthday party, at a dinner in his honor, the British novelist and playwright Somerset Maugham began his speech with these words: "There are many virtues in growing old." Then he paused for a long time, what seemed to be an eternity, and finally said, "I'm just trying to think what they are."

What's so good about getting old? When our bodies begin to fall apart and our minds take a hike? A pastor asked an elderly woman if she ever thought about the hereafter. "Oh, all the time," said the woman. "Every time I walk into a room I ask myself, Now what am I here after?" What's so good about getting old?

Paul says, "Our outer natures are wasting away." What's so good about that? As one writer put it, "You know you're getting old when almost everything hurts, and what doesn't hurt doesn't work any more." You know you're getting old when it feels like the morning after and you didn't even go anywhere the night before.

From Alzheimer's to arthritis to all kinds of aches and pains, what's so good about getting old? You are pushed aside, forgotten, used up, and generally not of much use to anyone anymore. Jay Leno made a joke of it all one night as he reported that the man who had created the Bic disposable pen and the Bic disposable razor had finally died. "At first," said Leno, "they were going to do a big funeral, but then decided to just throw him away."

Which is a parable in a way, isn't it, of what we do with those of chronological maturity? Earlier societies treated their aged with the utmost respect. Many looked to them for wisdom and advice. They really did as the Fifth Commandment says: They honored their fathers and their mothers. They built extra rooms on their houses to welcome them in. But we send them away and say, "Have a nice life, what there is left of it!" trying our best to remember to call and, if it's not too much trouble, to go by for a visit—at least on holidays. Of all the pains we as humans feel, the worst pain of all is feeling unneeded.

So Samuel is offered early retirement—early to him, that is, since he thought he had lots of energy and work left in him. But the people thought otherwise: "We want a king. We're tired of you." And they pushed him aside. Even the psalmist is worried: "Do not cast me off in the time of my old age, [O Lord]; do not forsake me when my strength is spent. . . . So even to old age and gray hairs, O God, do not forsake me . . ." (Ps. 70:9, 18a).

What's so good about getting old? At least three things I can think of this morning that are *existential, vocational,* and *spiritual.*

And the first is this: It's the fact that you're still alive. Consider the alternative! Some never make it to their later years. Their lives are cut off at a young age. Think of the young soldiers that hit the beaches of Normandy more than fifty years ago. Their average age was nineteen. Think how many thousands never got the chance to live full and complete lives as they made the ultimate sacrifice for their country and for the liberation of oppressed peoples in Europe. They never got the opportunity to experience all the joys of a long life.

My father reminisced with the children and grandchildren not long ago, telling his own stories of the Battle of the Bulge—many I had never heard before, perhaps because for so long they were too painful to tell—how buddies all around him were killed but somehow mysteriously he was spared, and how his dear mother prayed every day from Ps. 91:7: "A thousand may fall at your side, ten thousand at your right hand, but it will not come near you."

Some of you lived through that war or other wars and, thank God, you are still here. Think of all the wonderful memories you have of this whole life you have lived that you would never have known if a bullet had caught you instead of the ones on either side. What's so good about getting old, since it's both inevitable and irreversible, is that it beats the alternative.

There is an *existential* element to getting old that has to do with wisdom and maturity, if we have actually learned from our mistakes, that is. As for maturity, one writer suggests that we don't become more moral as we grow older; we just choose our sins more carefully. And one good thing about becoming ninety years old is that you're not subject to much peer pressure. So existentially, there are some good things about getting old.

But there are some good things *vocationally* as well, especially when you realize that some, like Arthur Becker, divide this period of life into three phases: the *young old,* the *middle old,* and the *frail elderly.*[1] I'm always a little leery of these phases of life categories that try to put us all into little cookie-cutter stages, like the one that says there are seven decades of human life from infancy to old age: Spills, Drills, Thrills, Bills, Ills, Pills, and Wills, which may be closer to the truth than we'd like to accept.

None of the categories is hard and fast, but generally the young old represents those from sixty-five to seventy-three, give or take up to five years on either side, those who are newly retired but "still very much in the prime of life although they are no longer engaged in full-time productive careers or occupations."[2] The young old "are still very vigorous and want to be active in the community, in the family, in the world, and in the church."[3] They retain this vigor in large measure by virtue of three things: continuation of service in church and community, good health, and financial stability.

According to experts those three—volunteer service, health, and finances—determine how long this period will last, and some actually "retain this healthful vigor" into their early eighties.

Others lose it as early as age sixty-eight because they have given up doing anything for others, or perhaps they have just slowed down for health or other reasons. That's the telling phrase of the middle old phase which usually describes those between seventy-three and eighty—the phrase is "slowing down." This can describe those who had very active lives in church and community. They still maintain a home and are still vital and alive, even enjoy travel and do not require hospitalization, but they have just slowed down. Some continue through this stage into their nineties, but then, eventually, many enter what is called the frail elderly phase, which comprises "most of the five percent of the population over 65 who live in nursing homes."[4] Though many are still mentally alert in this phase, they are no longer able to maintain homes or be as active as they once were.

But the good news of the scripture is that at whatever stage we find ourselves—young old, middle old, or frail elderly—God can still use us. Isn't that the whole purpose of the stories of Abraham and Sarah and Zechariah and Elizabeth having children when they were as good as dead? That God can use us no matter what our age or station in life? That God still has a purpose for us? The trick is figuring out what it is. So writes Robert Browning in "Rabbi Ben Ezra":

> Grow old along with me!
> The best is yet to be,
> The last of life, for which the first was made . . .
> Youth shows but half; trust God; see all, nor be afraid!

This is the time to do something for God since God has done so much for you. But what? Some believe that life ends at sixty-five. Others believe that's when it begins, and nothing will hold them back. So Michelangelo worked on St. Peter's Church at age seventy-one and began the Rondanini *Pietà* when he was nearly ninety. Verdi finished *Falstaff* at the age of eighty. Marc Chagall finished two murals for the Metropolitan Opera House in New York City at the age of seventy-seven. Jessica Tandy won the Oscar for best actress when she was eighty. Thomas Edison patented his last invention when he was eighty-one. And at the same age Benjamin Franklin completed the compromise for the adoption of the Constitution of the United States. At the age of ninety Duncan McClean won the world's Veteran Olympic Silver Medal in the 200-meter run. And at one hundred years of age George Abbott opened a play on Broadway and Grandma Moses illustrated "'Twas the Night before Christmas."

If you think God is through with you, you have another "think" coming. This really is, as the French call it, *troisième âge*, the third age. The important thing is to keep from turning bitter as we get older. A rabbi of a Conservative synagogue was asked in a Bible study how Solomon could have written Song of Songs, Proverbs, and Ecclesiastes. Sounds like a trick question. There were Orthodox and Conservative and some Reform Jews in the Bible study. He thought for a moment and said, "Solomon wrote Song of Songs in his youth, Proverbs in middle age, and Ecclesiastes when he had turned bitter in old age." Whatever we think of that biblical interpretation, how sad it is that we might turn bitter in our later years instead of seeing what we can now do for God, sharing our wisdom and our experience with younger ones. When we have lived a whole life of faith we should end it not in despair, but in hope and joy as we keep believing in God and keep doing something for others as long as we have breath, whether it be offering a kind word or just saying a prayer.

My Grandmother Correy, a spirited woman at ninety-one, finally moved into Methodist Manor in Tulsa, Oklahoma, not long before she died. Always full of life. Gave up mowing her lawn only a couple of years before that. Not long before she died, she was entering that frail elderly phase but not giving up. She figured that God still had some use for her. One day she noticed a woman who sat at dinner with a scowl. She never talked. Every day, Grandmother would try to strike up a conversation. But those around her said, "Don't try. She doesn't want to be bothered." Well, to hear that was a challenge to my grandmother. So she went back over to the woman. And the woman just scowled. "I don't talk!" said the woman finally. "You don't have to," said my grandmother, "I talk enough for both of us!" Everyone else was smiling and talking, but the woman just sat there scowling. Again, they all told my grandmother, "You're wasting your time. She doesn't talk." But then one day, to everyone's shock and surprise, this woman actually smiled and she began to talk, like a scene from the movie *The Awakening*.

Don't you see? God still has something for you and me to do and we experience God's providence existentially and vocationally, but most of all spiritually. For as Paul says, even as our outer nature is wasting away, our inner nature is being renewed each day. As our physical and mental faculties wane, we are not just sliding down the slippery slope to an ignominious death; we are climbing ever higher and higher into the presence of God. William Barclay is right when he says that we need not fear the years for they bring us nearer, not to death, but to God and to our loved ones.

In a little fishing village in Northern Ireland, a Mrs. Bunting, well over eighty years of age, said to her minister, "Pastor, I'm not afraid to die because I have a claim in heaven." What was her claim? It was her own child who had died in infancy, and even though Mrs. Bunting had lived to be a ripe old age, all the time she had loved that little one. She wasn't afraid to die because there was something of her waiting in heaven.[5]

Is that what we see as we approach that time when we are about to die? Pastors, friends, and loved ones see it all the time with those whose "diminishing physical strength" is accompanied by "increasing spiritual vitality."[6] "As their bodies" fail, their spirits burn all the more brightly, and there is a "kind of luminosity about them" that is "marvelously impressive and appealing." Somehow they have discovered and taught us that there is a glory in the morning and "the evening, too, has a splendour of its own. It was Sir William Mulock, Chief Justice of Canada, who said on his ninetieth birthday, 'I am still at work with my face to the future. The shadows of evening lengthen . . . but the morning is in my heart. . . . The testimony I bear is this, the best of life is further on, hidden from our eyes beyond the hills of Time.'"[7]

Shakespeare is right, isn't he, when he says, "All's well that ends well." The question is, No matter how young or old you are, how are you preparing for the end of your life?

Let us pray. Eternal God: you have led us through our days and years, made wisdom ripe and faith mature. Show us your purpose for our lives, so that, when youth is spent, we may not find life empty or labor stale, but may devote ourselves to dear loves and worthy tasks, with undiminished strength.

Your love for us never ends, O God, even when by age or weakness we can no longer work. When we retire, keep us awake to your will for us. Give us energy to enjoy the world, to attend to neighbors busy people neglect, and to contribute wisely of our time and resources to the life of the church. If we can offer nothing but our prayers, remind us that our prayers are a useful work, so that we may live always serving Jesus Christ, our hope and true joy.

Almighty God: by your power Jesus Christ was raised from death. Watch over dying men and women. Fill eyes with light, to see beyond human sight a home within your love, where pain is gone and frail flesh turns to glory. Banish fear. Brush tears away. Let death be gentle as nightfall, promising a day when songs of joy shall make us glad to be together with Jesus Christ who lives in triumph, the Lord of life eternal.[8]

# 2

# Aging:
# A Long Loving Look at the Real

*Walter J. Burghardt, S.J.*

For anyone in a developed country who lives a normal number of years, aging is inevitable. Not just growing older, but growing old, experiencing that for which we have long had only a frightening term: old age.[1] No single definition of old age spans the universe: It begins much earlier in Burundi than in Britain. For our present purposes, let me describe aging in a way that stresses the experience and outlook of developed countries. Old age sets in when I sense that, after the usual periods of adolescence, young adulthood, and middle age, I am reaching the last significant stage of my life. Call it the winter of human existence. Assume, with some recognized scholars, that it begins at roughly sixty to sixty-five. In that context I shall (1) suggest some of the more serious problems the aging and aged face, (2) touch broadly on the Christian vision of aging, and (3) propose in some detail a perhaps surprising antidote not only to counteract the distressful aspects of dying but also to sketch a spirituality of aging uncommonly dear to my heart. I shall end with a handful of swift suggestions for those who are privileged to preach to men and women of the third age.

## Problems

Even in the very best of situations—health and wealth, happiness and a host of devoted friends—aging demands profound reflection. I must face up to Erik Erikson's key polarity: integration versus despair. Somehow I must make peace with my flawed existence, must grasp my life as something whole. To continue creative, I must retain my link to youthful vitality, my tie to the forces of growth in myself and in my world. I must come to terms with suffering: a body that is breaking down, illnesses to which aging flesh and spirit are especially heir. I must confront death: my own and the almost daily demise of dear ones. Only then can I live old age without bitterness. Otherwise the third age will prove to be only the winter of my discontent.[2]

In the United States, aging is complexified by a cultural phenomenon: the ideal of senior citizenship America has fashioned. We inhabit a culture that extols the young and the restless, the bold and the beautiful. The ideal of aging? To seem ageless. A wondrous wedding of Clark Gable and Grandma Moses, Pablo Picasso and Susan B. Anthony, Maurice Chevalier and Marlene Dietrich, Paul Newman and Queen Elizabeth II.

Perhaps the most critical aspect of this problem is that the controlling culture considers the elderly literally "useless." The aged rarely serve a practical purpose; they don't "do" anything. They are irrelevant to big business, big government, big labor, big military, big education. The "new boys [and girls] on the block," economic man and economic woman, draw their knowledge and wisdom from computers, not from tradition; from the creative imagination of the young and the restless, not from the hoary stories of the aging. Increasingly the young drive the senior partners into early retirement. Moreover, the elderly are a drain on the economy. They use up medical resources, medical miracles, that could benefit the "useful" members of society; the young are burdened with support of the old. Already doctors are toying with lethal injections not only for the irretrievably comatose but for so many in intolerable pain or simply weary of living. Decades ago Simone de Beauvoir phrased the problem in a more general context with pungent brevity:

> Apart from some exceptions, the old man no longer *does* anything. He is defined by an *exis*, not by a *praxis*: a being, not a doing. Time is carrying him towards an end—death—which is not *his* and which is not postulated or laid down by any project. This is why he looks to active members of the community like one of a "different species," one in whom they do not recognize themselves.[3]

By contrast, it is instructive to study the outlook on aging in various religions of the world.[4] Instructive to uncover the insight of southern Ghana's Akans: Knowledge is power, but aging is wisdom—a wisdom that calls for reverence, for respect. Instructive to resonate to the woodland Ojibway as they reflect the tradition of Native Americans in their insistence, "Honor the aged; in honoring them you have life and wisdom." Instructive to learn that for Confucius filial piety, respect for elders, is the supreme principle of morality, for it can define the very meaning of our being in this world, is a powerful binding force that produces a stable society, is a source of world peace and order. Instructive to see the Hindu tradition refusing to focus on the physical weakness and disabilities of the elderly, stressing instead their spiritual maturity and wisdom, which command universal respect and reveal them as models of an authentic human life serving all humanity disinterestedly. Instructive to hear the Buddha admonishing his followers to treat parents as a living Buddha. How keen of Buddhists to regard aging as not diminishment but increase, a movement toward fuller life, neither a downward spiral toward dissolution nor a triumphal procession to glory and immortality. Even the debilitating aspects of aging are a gift, because they put the aging in direct contact with the truth of their existence.

Profoundly impressive is the biblical tradition of the Prior Testament and rabbinic reflection thereon, for there human living is governed by a theology of Presence.[5] Mortal creatures, "nothing but dust and ashes" (Gen. 18:27), exist in creative partnership with God, "little less than God" (Ps. 8:5). Living in God's presence dictates the way they act in other relationships. Relating to God's presence in awe and love (the biblical expression for religion), they are motivated to similar reverence in human interaction.

Reflecting their awe of God, the younger are to "rise before the aged and defer to the old" (Lev. 19:32). With reverential posture and respectful speech, they acknowledge the dignity and worth of the aged somewhat as they receive the presence of God. Such reverence stems from a realization that parents, like God, are creators. "One relates to parents by the fact of birth, to his teachers and the learned by his reception of wisdom and to the aged by their achievement of experiential knowledge."[6] The aging transmit to the younger their experience of the past—not as sheer knowledge but as a living witness to God's presence. Because life is a gift of God and all moments of life are equally sacred, the period of deterioration in aging demands special concern. Every effort must be exerted—legally, socially, medically—to preserve the life of those who are facing death, and to preserve it in dignity. Reverence before God-given life—such is Jewry's precious bequest to the nations.

Aging Hebrews themselves are not to see in the passage of time simply defeat, punishment, irreversible decline. "Aging can mean growth, a celebration, the sanctification of time, an opportunity once again for experiencing the presence which makes us truly human,"[7] for pursuing righteousness, like Abraham, in imitation of God. Every sensitive man and woman must listen in awe as the revered rabbi Abraham Joshua Heschel appeals touchingly to contemporary society, as he insists that the elderly need not only recreation but a vision, require not only a memory but a dream; as he proclaims that simply to be alive is holy.[8]

## Christian Vision

Precisely here the Christian vision, if not every Christian, declares a resounding dissent from the dominant American culture, a rousing reaffirmation of the Jewish insight, "Just to be is a blessing, just to live is holy." Understandably, with certain specifically Christian emphases. Save for the unalterably comatose or the hopelessly senile or demented, there is no person alive who is "finished," who has reached either perfection or the limit of his or her striving. A Christian is, from womb to tomb, a pilgrim. Not simply because on this earth we have no lasting city, but more pertinently because Christian existence is a ceaseless effort to follow Christ, and that struggle never ends this side of the grave

This following of Christ is not slavish imitation, copying the life of Jesus in its details. We live out our faith, hope, and love in ways that in his restricted life Jesus did not and could not experience. He was a man, not a woman; he was a teacher, but not a scholar; he did not experience old age or Alzheimer's disease. He never even lived to be a Jesuit!

More accurate, then, than "imitate" is "follow," be Jesus' disciple. And if you ask where concretely, for any and every Christian, independently of time and circumstance, Jesus is to be followed, we must answer with German theologian Karl Rahner: "The Christian, every Christian at all times, follows Jesus by *dying* with him; following Jesus has its ultimate truth and reality and universality in the following of the Crucified."[9]

But following the Crucified, following Jesus in our dying, is not limited to the close of our earthbound existence, to the terminal cancer, the cardiac arrest. Dying in a theological sense begins when living begins; we share in Jesus' dying by sharing his cross through the whole of our lives. Whatever makes for pain—pain of flesh or of spirit—should be part and parcel of our Christian dying. Diverticula or disappointments, schizophrenia or the wrenching of my heart, dying hopes or the death of a dear one, the insecurities of youth and the trembling of the aging—whatever it is that pricks our pride, assails our lustiness, intimates our mortality, takes the joy from our very bones, in all these brief moments of what Rahner called "dying in installments" we confront a question: How do we cope? Protest? Despair? Become cynical? Cling all the more desperately to what has not yet been taken from us? Or accept with Christlike obedience this "promise of an eternal Christmas full of light, regard slight breakdowns as events of grace"?[10]

This dying into Christ demands as an essential ingredient a kenosis, a self-emptying akin to Christ's own in taking our flesh. But kenosis is not a virtue we request from the Lord on retiring from active existence. If old age is to be genuinely Christian, a progressively more intense following of one Master, then all through life we have to "let go." Let go of where we've been, let go of the level of life where we are now, so as to live more fully. Let go of childhood and adolescence, of good looks and youthful energy, of familiar places and beloved faces, of a high-paying job and human applause. Not simply because we have no choice. Rather because only by letting go of yesterday can we grow more fully into Christ today. We the aged do not *forget* our yesterdays; we simply dare not *live* in them.

## Contemplation

These reflections lead into my third and most significant point: a proposal for the aging that is rarely if ever offered, even though it not only can counteract certain distressful aspects of dying but involves a realistic spirituality splendidly attuned to men and women who no longer "do" anything.

My proposal is . . . contemplation. The contemplative Carmelite William McNamara once called it "a pure intuition of being, born of love. It is experiential awareness of reality and a way of entering into immediate communion with reality." And what is reality?

> People, trees, lakes, mountains. You can study things, but unless
> you enter into this intuitive communion with them, you can only
> know *about* them, you don't *know* them. To take a long loving look
> at something—a child, a glass of wine, a beautiful meal—this is a
> natural act of contemplation, of loving admiration.

The problem? "All the way through school we are taught to abstract; we are not taught loving awareness."[11]

An exciting definition: a long loving look at the real.[12] Each word is crucial: real . . . look . . . long . . . loving. The *real* is not some intangible deity in outer space. Reality is living, pulsing people; reality is rain and rainbow; reality is the sun setting in ruddy splendor over the Swiss Alps, a gentle doe streaking through the Catskills; reality is a sparkling glass of Burgundy, Mozart's *Missa solemnis*, a child lapping a chocolate ice-cream cone; reality is a striding woman with wind-blown hair; reality is the dying/rising Christ. Contrary to common conjecture, what I contemplate is never some philosophical abstraction, where a leaf is no longer green, water no longer ripples, God no longer smiles. It is always what is most real: what philosophers call the concrete singular.

This real I *look* at. I do not analyze or argue it, describe or define it; I am one with it. I do not move around it; I enter into it. Lounging by a stream, I do not exclaim "Ah, yes, $H_2O$!" I simply let the water trickle gently through my fingers. Loving awareness. I do not theologize about Calvary, about its redemptive significance; I link a pierced hand to mine. Walter Kerr once compared contemplation to falling in love: "the single, simple vibration that gives us such joy in the meeting of eyes or the lucky conjunction of interchanged words. Something private and singular and uniquely itself is touched—and known in the touching."[13] To "look" wholly means that my whole person reacts. Not only my mind, but my eyes and ears, smelling and touching and tasting; yes, emotions and passions. Far more openness, far more letting go, than we were permitted of old, in a more severe spirituality, where, for example, touch was "out," because touch is dangerous. No one ever thought to remind us that free will is even more dangerous. Or cold reason.

This look at the real is a *long* look. Not in terms of measured time, but wonderfully unhurried, gloriously unharried. (For the "retired," perhaps the first opportunity in a lifetime.) To contemplate is to rest—to rest in the real. Not lifelessly or languidly, not sluggishly or inertly. My entire being is alive, incredibly responsive, vibrating to every throb of the real. For once, time is irrelevant. You do not time the Philharmonic, you do not clock the Last Supper. Neither should you put a stopwatch on loving awareness—of a dear one, of a rose in bloom, of Christ in the garden of his agony or on his final cross.

But this long look must be a *loving* look. Not a fixed stare, not the long look of a Judas. Contemplation demands that the real captivate me, hold me imprisoned, at times delight me. Tchaikovsky's *Swan Lake* or Spaghetti Bolognese, the grace of God's swans or the compassion in the eyes of Christ—whatever or whoever the real, contemplation calls forth love, one-ness with the other. For contemplation is not study, not cold examination, not a computer. To contemplate is to be in love.

Granted, contemplation does not always summon up delight. The real includes sin and war, poverty and racism, illness and death. The real is AIDS and apartheid, Down's syndrome and MS, bloated bellies and stunted minds, respirators and last gasps. But even here the real I contemplate must end in compassion, and compassion that mimics Christ is a synonym for love.

A long loving look at the real. From such contemplation comes com-munion. I mean the discovery of the Holy in deep, thoughtful encoun-ters—with God's creation, with God's people, with God's self. Thus is fashioned what the second-century bishop Irenaeus called "God's glory—man/woman alive!" To age like this is to be alive as never before.

But how do you actualize this capacity for contemplation? Five swift suggestions. First, some sort of desert experience. Not necessarily a phys-ical desert. Not so much a place as an experience that takes hold of you, that brings you face to face with solitude, with vastness, even with powers of life and death beyond your control. Remember Jesus in the garden of his agony, of his aloneness, with his special friends asleep nearby; Jesus afraid, begging his father "Don't let me die," his sweat "like great drops of blood falling down upon the ground" (Luke 22:44), needing an angel from heaven to strengthen him for the trial before him. At some point all of us, old as well as young, must face Nikos Kazantzakis's terrifying trinity: "love, death, and God—perhaps one and the same."

Second, develop a feeling for festivity. Here I recommend Josef Pieper's slender volume *In Tune with the World: A Theory of Festivity.*[14] Pieper de-velops the thesis that festivity resides in activity that is meaningful in itself, not tied to goals, to "so that" or "in order to." Live the present moment, enjoy this experience, this fresh face of the real, as if nothing else existed. Such festivity calls for renunciation: I must take usable time and withdraw it from utility. And this I must do out of love, whose expression is joy. Festivity is a yes to the world, to the reality of things, to the existence of woman and man; it is a yes to the world's Creator. It is only if I can say such a festive yes to the real that I will sense, with Teilhard de Chardin, how "God is as outstretched and tangible as the atmosphere in which we are bathed."

Third, encourage a sense of "play." I don't mean "fooling around." I mean what poet Francis Thompson meant when, in his essay on Shelley, he likened the poet's gifts to a child's faculty of make-believe, but raised to the nth power—whose box of toys is the universe, who "makes bright mischief with the moon," in whose hand "the meteors nuzzle their noses."

It demands a sense of wonder. With that sense we are born; but as we grow older, most of us lose it. We get blasé and worldly-wise and sophisticated, no longer run our fingers through water, shout at the stars, make faces at the moon. We've grown up. Rabbi Heschel saw it as our contemporary trap: "believing that everything can be explained, that reality is a simple affair which has only to be organized in order to be mastered. All enigmas can be solved, and all wonder is nothing but 'the effect of novelty upon ignorance.'"[15]

No, dear third-age friend, don't put everything under a microscope, don't program life in a computer. Let your imagination loose to play with ideas—what it means to be alive, to be in love, to believe and to hope. Reach for the wild idea!

Fourth, don't try to "possess" the object of your delight, whether divine or human, imprisoned marble or free-flowing rivulet. Here Walter Kerr has written a paragraph that profoundly influences my own aging:

> To regain some delight in ourselves and in our world, we are forced to abandon, or rather to reverse, an adage. A bird in the hand is *not* worth two in the bush—unless one is an ornithologist, the curator of the Museum of Natural History, or one of those Italian vendors who supply restaurants with larks. A bird in the hand is no longer a bird at all: it is a specimen; it may be dinner. Birds are birds only when they are in the bush or on the wing; their worth as birds can be known only at a discreet and generous distance.[16]

A fifth suggestion: Read, make friends with, remarkable men and women who have themselves looked long and lovingly at the real. The list is long and impressive. For the moment, think only of some personal favorites of mine. I mean biblical figures like Abraham and Mary of Nazareth, murmuring yes to Yahweh though they knew not where it would take them, knew only that it was God who was calling. I mean modern martyrs like Martin Luther King, with a dream of black freedom he bathed in blood. I mean Lao-tzu doing everything through being, Rabbi Heschel doing everything through worship. I mean philosophers like Jacques Maritain, insisting that the high point of knowledge is not an idea but an experience: Man/woman "feels" God. I mean uncanonized saints like Dorothy Day and Mother Teresa, arms embracing the homeless and the hopeless from New York to Calcutta. I mean Thomas Merton, always the contemplative but moving from renunciation to involvement, making contact with Hindu and Buddhist and Sufi, protesting Vietnam and violence, racial injustice and nuclear war. I mean Anne Morrow Lindbergh, with her countercultural response to friends (expressed so sensitively in *Gift from the Sea*), "I cannot come. This is my hour to be alone."

These, and so many others, are not solitaries, not neurotic escapists, but flesh and blood in a flesh-and-blood world—unique, however, because each in his or her way looked long and lovingly at the real. Touch men and women like these, learn from them, and aging will prove an absorbing adventure—an adventure in coming alive.

What is it, in summary, that I would say to my contemporaries in aging? Good aging friends, our American culture needs you, needs me. But only if the younger—economic man and economic woman—can discover in us what it means to be genuinely alive. Only if, in looking at us, they discover men and women not only grayer and more wrinkled but living more fully, more joyously, than they—more fully, more joyously, than we ourselves have ever lived before. Very simply, only if they see in us what second-century Bishop Irenaeus of Lyons expressed so pithily: "God's glory—women and men alive!"

## Suggestions for the Preacher

Henri Nouwen has penetrated to the heart of the matter: how the elderly can teach the teacher, preach to the preacher.

> Our first question is not how to go out and help the elderly, but how to allow the elderly to enter into the center of our own lives, how to create the space where they can be heard and listened to from within with careful attention. Quite often our concern to preach, teach, or cure prevents us from perceiving and receiving what those we care for have to offer.
>
> Thus care for the elderly means, first of all, to make ourselves available to the experience of becoming old. Only he who has recognized the relativity of his own life can bring a smile to the face of a man who feels the closeness of death. In that sense, caring is first a way to our own aging self, where we can find the healing powers for all those who share in the human condition.[17]

Once preachers have allowed the aging into their own lives, have opened themselves to the experience of aging (whatever their age), have listened as if their own lives are at stake (as they indeed are), then the actual preaching is far less fearsome. Why? Because the gap, the abyss, that yawns so often between preacher and listener has been narrowed significantly. It is no longer the younger, the healthier, the energetic mouthing from a pulpit moldy panaceas purloined from encyclopedias on aging. The preacher is now on a level with, perhaps a step below, his or her congregation, is sharing some of the wisdom that has been gathered from the congregation, infusing it with the insights of God's own word.

Then the stories will flow, some humorous, some tearful—stories from the storehouse of the aging. Then the symbols (signs that suggest more than they can explicitly say) will be splendidly pertinent. Not always the preacher's own preferred symbols. Not Michael Jackson, an Acura, a Big Mac, but Mother Teresa, a grandchild's crib, a God who smiles lovingly from a cross. Then the imagination will break loose, find rich meaning not only in the razzle-dazzle of Super Bowls and the Dow Jones, but in the simple tales that keep the past alive in the present. Then the scriptures, Prior Testament and New, will speak to the preacher with fresh force: Abraham leaving home and kindred at seventy-five; Sirach's "Do not disregard the discourse of the aged" (Sirach 8:9); the octogenarian prophetess Anna coming upon the child Jesus in the temple (Luke 2:36–38); the risen Jesus predicting to Peter, "When you are old, you will stretch out your hands, and another will gird you and carry you where you do not wish to go" (John 21:18)—a host of passages that will make new sense to second age as well as third.

The secret? Listen: to the aging and to the Lord who never ages.

### SERMON

# Aging, Changing, Giving

## Walter J. Burghardt, S.J.

*Occasion for sermon:* This homily was preached at the annual Mass for members of Catholic Seniors Clubs of Nassau County, Long Island, New York, held at St. Frances de Chantal Church, Wantagh, New York, April 22, 1993. The scripture readings were Rev. 12:1–12 and Luke 1:26–38.

Your celebration centers on a significant monosyllable: change. Change can be frightening: I've lost my job. Change can be welcome: My hiatal hernia has stopped mimicking a heart attack. It can be challenging: I have a chance to contribute something new to society. In the context of this eucharistic gathering, let me focus on change in our Catholic existence. Three stages to my development: (1) change in the church; (2) our Lady's response to change; (3) change as it touches you and me.

## I

First, change in the church. It happens, you know. The church changes—in the way it thinks, in the way it worships, in the way it lives. I don't mean that the church ceases to be what Christ intended it to be. I do mean that the church—the pope included—grows in understanding. Understanding what God has revealed to us in Christ; understanding how our sacraments can better serve our people; understanding what it means to live morally in a whole new technological age.

Several concrete examples. Vatican II startled many a Catholic when it declared that the grace of Christ is at work, richly and incessantly, not only within individual Protestants but with the community called Protestant, suggested strongly that the bonds that unite us (for example, living faith, fruitful baptism) link us not only as individuals but more importantly as communities. Rome surprised many a Catholic when it turned our altars around, changed a centuries-old Latin into our native tongues, allowed us to enfold the body of Christ within our hands. Not only don't we encourage any longer the burning of heretics; not only has the church moved forward on organ transplantation. The church and its theologians are newly struggling to decide if and when we may withhold nutrition from a patient in a permanently vegetative state.

The point of these examples? The church of Christ does change, has to change. Why? Because to stand still is to die; because Christ wants the church to grow, as he grew, not only in age but in wisdom. But not to worry! Led by the Spirit through trial and error, through fortune and misfortune, the church retains its identity, remains the church of Christ.

## II

Second, our Lady's response to change. As I grew up early in our century, many of us had a childlike conception of Jesus' mother: a sweet teenager surprised by joy in Nazareth; a young mother cradling her infant in a stable warmed by friendly animals; a dutiful wife to Joseph in Nazareth; a somewhat worried mother searching for her twelve-year-old in Jerusalem; a sorrowful mother standing silently beneath the cross of her only child.

Nothing false about those pictures. Still, they do not represent the reality that gives them her profound life. What is that reality? Change—radical change. This girl was to change in a moment from a Jewish teenager indistinguishable from her playmates to a unique young lady pregnant with God's only Son, in danger of being stoned to death in accordance with Jewish law. This young lady changed into an unusual mother: while pregnant she had to leave her native Nazareth for Bethlehem eighty-five miles away, could find no decent room there, gave birth where only brute animals gave birth. This mother had to live with agony when she lost her twelve-year-old boy in Jerusalem: "Child, why have you treated us like this? Look, your father and I have been terribly worried and have been searching for you" (Luke 2:48). And she "did not understand" his explanation (v. 50). This mother experienced change when her fellow Nazarenes, who "spoke well of [Jesus] and were amazed at the gracious words that came from his mouth" (Luke 4:22), suddenly turned on him and tried to "hurl him off [a] cliff" (v. 29). This mother had to cope with change when Jesus' own relatives "went out to restrain him, for people were saying, 'He has gone out of his mind'" (Mark 3:21). This mother had to watch helplessly while soldiers stripped him, pinned him to a cross between two robbers, and gambled for his garments, while the people he loved jeered at him, taunted him to come down from the cross. This mother had to cradle her lifeless Son in her arms, place his cold flesh in a tomb, and hope that his Father would raise him from the dead.

Yes, hope. Always hope, rooted in faith. For no angel gave our Lady a script for Jesus' life, a scenario for his dying. No angel told this Jewish girl about the Trinity, about a Son who was equal in every respect to the Father of us all. No angel explained his leaving her from a criminal's cross. No angel told her, "Not to worry, Mary! Come around Sunday and you'll find an empty tomb."

The point of all this? For our Lady, too, to change was to grow, to become more and more like her Son. Our Lady could live with change, with radical change, with deathly change, because she lived to perfection the response to God she first spoke to Gabriel: "Let it be with me as you say" (Luke 1:38). She was Jesus' first and perfect disciple; for she it was who lived more remarkably than any other sheerly human person Jesus' definition of disciples: "those who hear the word of God and do it" (Luke 8:21).

### III

This brings me to my third point: change as it touches you and me. Most of us here have passed from adolescence, from young adulthood, from middle age to a generation for which America has a frightening term: old age. We inhabit a culture that canonizes youth and beauty, activity and productivity, power and sexual prowess. If you are eternally young and ceaselessly attractive, if after sixty or sixty-five you continue your career with little letdown and still make an impact on an acre of God's world, if you can jog or play squash or straddle a Honda, if you can still satisfy a man or woman sexually, then your aging is ideal. In fact, you're not growing old at all! The ideal is a compound of Bob Hope and Eva Gabor, Ronald Reagan and Mother Teresa, George Burns and Katharine Hepburn, Cary Grant and Lauren Bacall. The only ideal of senior citizen we accept in America is an aging without change or limits or loss.

Not so the Christian vision. Here you and I are as important as Michael Jordan and Bill Clinton, as Madonna and Barbra Streisand, as Joe Montana and Princess Diana. For our ideal is the resounding call of St. Paul to the Christians of Philippi in Macedonia:

> I regard everything as loss because of the surpassing value of knowing Christ Jesus my Lord. For his sake I have suffered the loss of all things, . . . in order that I may gain Christ and be found in him. . . . I want to know Christ and the power of his resurrection and the sharing of his sufferings. . . . This one thing I do: forgetting what lies behind and straining forward to what lies ahead, I press on toward the goal. (Phil. 3:8–14)

"Forgetting what lies behind." You and I are not doomed to live in the past. We are to live today and tomorrow. For our task is to grow—grow into what Paul called "full-grown adulthood." And what is that? The fullness of Christ (Eph. 4:13). "Speaking the truth in love, we must grow up in every way . . . into Christ" (v. 15).

So then, our maturity, our fullness, lies ahead of us. That maturing process can hardly be spelled out in a homily. Let me focus on one area where you and I can, perhaps must, grow into Christ, an area that is increasingly critical in our society, is intimately linked to Catholic Charities and our Offices of Justice and Peace. Paul has suggested it: "speaking the truth in love." Better still, living the truth in love. It is a vivid way of saying that your Catholicism and mine should be a faith that does justice. Here justice turns into love. For the justice that the Old Testament prophets proclaimed, the justice that Jesus preached as his own reason for taking our flesh, is not simply an ethical concept: giving to others what they deserve, because they are human persons, because they have rights that can be proven from philosophy or have been written into law. Biblical justice is treating our sisters and brothers as our covenant with God demands. We are to father the fatherless and mother the motherless, feed the famished and shelter the homeless, clothe the naked and visit the housebound and imprisoned, because this implements the second great commandment of the law and the gospel: We are to love our sisters and brothers as if we were standing in their shoes, love each person like another I. In fact, we are to love every other as Jesus loves us—and that means, even unto crucifixion.

Our times demand it. For we live in an age that some sociologists describe as a resurgence of late–nineteenth-century rugged individualism, where what ultimately matters is the one-and-only I, where there is only so much water in the well and I had better get there first, where the race is to the swift, the shrewd, the savage, and the devil take the hindmost. A paradoxical country where one out of every five children grows up hungry, crack and coke ravage the flesh and savage the minds of our teens, a million youngsters sleep on our streets each night, racial hatred bubbles beneath the surface of our cities, elderly men and women rummage in garbage cans for the food we discard so lightly, 37 million Americans have no realistic access to health care.

In our stress on youth and strength, on computers and dollars, we have neglected an incredibly rich resource. These tortured sisters and brothers of yours need you, need your love, need to hear your warm voice, see the compassion in your eyes, profit from your experience of joy and sorrow, of love exchanged and love amid the ruins. You need not walk alone; the organizations exist, are there, within walking distance. If we Catholics were to mobilize our "third age" men and women, organize them to confront the ills of our country, send them out in pairs like the original disciples, we could change the face of this land.

Not all of you can walk the streets, raise up the fallen, speak the truth in love. And yet, no one of you is powerless. Listen to inspired St. Paul: "[The Lord] said to me, 'My grace is sufficient for you, for my power is made perfect in weakness.' So, I will boast all the more gladly of my weaknesses, so that the power of Christ may dwell in me. Therefore I am content with weaknesses . . . for the sake of Christ; for whenever I am weak, then I am strong" (2 Cor. 12:9–10). "I can do all things through him who strengthens me" (Phil. 4:13). The power behind those who walk and talk is the hidden army that suffers and prays. Never underestimate that power. Suffering and prayer brought an angel from heaven to strengthen Jesus in the hour when he was sweating blood, afraid to die.

Good friends in Christ: I who share your years and tears can promise you one gift with supreme confidence. Get involved with even one person who experiences more of Christ's crucifixion than of his resurrection, and the change in your own life will amaze you. Many of you have already experienced it. I can only hope and pray that every single one of you will. For your own sake, for the sake of your bleeding church, for the sake of your tortured land. In your "third age" apostolate, God lead you, God feed you, God speed you.

# 3

# Threescore, Ten, and Trouble:
# A Biblical View of Aging

*David G. Buttrick*

What an assignment—a chapter on "the Bible and aging." The topic has become something of a joke in our house: "You're going to talk about aging?" my wife asked, one eyebrow lifted quizzically. "Well," said she with a broad smirk, "you qualify!" Indeed I do, for I have tipped past sixty-five. Though statistics speak of an extended life span, and AARP lists discounts for senior citizens, for most human beings the so-called Golden Age is something of a pain in the neck—often quite literally. So what does the Bible say about old age? What does the Bible say to the young, who may or may not know what on earth to do with their youth? What does the Bible say to those with gray hair who have begun to timetable their life spans? Our topic: the biblical view of aging.

## Old Age as an Issue

These days aging is a hot issue. More, aging is now a disturbing, cash-down social issue. At the turn of the century, only around 4 percent of the population was over sixty-five. A few years from now, when we reach the year 2000, the elderly will represent better than 13 percent of the population.[1] And then, by 2030, the elderly will top 20 percent of the citizenship.[2] The average life span is now about seventy-five. So there are more older Americans needing support these days. Social Security and Medicare funds have become, year after year, a bigger chunk of the national budget. Once upon a time, Indians in the New Mexican pueblos would simply add another adobe room, attaching space for the elderly. But these days, simple solutions are no longer possible. Will we have to build centers for the elderly in all our villages; apartments, care units, special hospitals? And if we do provide for the aging, will the tax burden be insupportable? For those who are aging the issues are personal—What's going to happen to me? But for all of us, the problem of the elderly looms as a social conundrum to be brooded by social scientists, economists, not to mention troubled members of Congress.

Of course, the issue is singularly urgent for Jewish and Christian faith communities. After all, we believe we are called to display God's justice and love to the world—we must be holy as God is holy. The Fifth Commandment speaks God's word to us, "Honor your father and your mother, so that your days may be long in the land that the LORD your God is giving you" (Ex. 20:12). Inasmuch as we pray together, "Your will be done," obviously we must find ways to do the commandment of God. Because all the commandments have social dimension, we must do the will of God as a "light of the world," showing a way to the nation in which we live, indeed to the whole wide world. Care of the elderly should not be simply a family matter among us, for, in a way, Christian community replaces the conventional family unit; Christian community is a new-order family. Therefore, congregations must begin to wrestle with the problem of aging members. We are called to do God's love and justice with the world's elderly people.[3]

## How Old Is Old?

Let's begin by asking an odd question: What are we talking about? Exactly what is old age in the Bible? What does the Bible mean by the elderly? On the one hand, we get exaggerated ages reported for cult heroes—did Abraham actually live to 175 or Methuselah to 969?[4] On the other hand, we must realize that actually the average life span in biblical times was not long. Bundle all the kings of Israel together and figure their life span; they average no longer than forty-four years of age and, of course, they were cared for and protected.[5] For most people, we must guess that an average life expectancy was twenty to thirty years, that better than half the population probably did not make it to "thirtysomething." As a result old age in biblical times must have begun in the forties, and sixty years was positively a venerable old age.[6] Psalm 90 is explicit:

> The days of our life are seventy years,
> or perhaps eighty, if we are strong;
> even then, their span is only toil and trouble;
> they are soon gone, and we fly away.

In all likelihood, the psalm is remarkably optimistic; few people in biblical times would have achieved seventy, and fewer still eighty—what we call old age these days would have been a miracle in biblical times. No doubt Willard Scott, NBC's geriatric weatherman, who hands out kudos to one-hundred-year-oldsters, would have been out of work in the biblical world. Of course, even when venerable old age was achieved, it was scarcely as sweet as is portrayed. Again and again, there is a splendid realism in the

Bible, as for example, when Barzillai the Gileadite turns down an honorary cabinet position with King David, saying:

> Today I am eighty years old; can I discern what is pleasant and what is not? Can your servant taste what he eats or what he drinks? Can I still listen to [i.e., distinguish] the voices of singing men and singing women? Then why should your servant be an added burden to my lord the king? (2 Sam. 19:35)

Life was short in biblical times, and if it wasn't short, it soon weakened, tumbling toward the ultimate sub-zero of shadowy Sheol. Old age began early in those days.

For some reason, the Hebrew Bible describes aging with the symbol of hair. The elderly are called "gray heads" or, sometimes, if white, they are "wool"-haired.[7] So old age involved turning gray. Another common disability was a dimness of sight and of hearing. While Moses at more than a hundred years of age had unimpaired vision according to Deuteronomy (34:7) and absolutely no loss of vigor, he was obviously an exception to the rule. By contrast, according to First Samuel, the priest Eli's eyes "had begun to grow dim so that he could not see" (1 Sam. 3:2). And Qoheleth, the dour preacher of Ecclesiastes, sums up blind and deaf old age metaphorically: "the moon and the stars are darkened," he says, "and all the daughters of song are brought low." Old age in the Bible is depicted as an enlarging physical weakness, constricting life. The elderly are no longer strong: Proverbs tells us that "the glory of youths is their strength, but the beauty of the aged is their gray hair" (20:29), but most of the aging would gladly trade their gray heads for youthful energies.

The most distressing sign of aging in the Hebrew Bible is the loss of sexual power. Qoheleth describes old age bluntly, "The grasshopper drags itself along, and the aphrodisiacs fail" (Eccl. 12:2–5, my translation). Apparently, the caperberry, which was regarded as an aphrodisiac, no longer seemed to stimulate sexual desire.[8] Old age in scripture appears to be measured in a pleasantly earthy fashion, by sexuality; that is, not only the ability to enjoy sex but the potency to impregnate. So Sarah, when promised a son in her old age, laughs her head off, but then she asks wryly, "After I have grown old, and my husband is old, shall I have pleasure?" (Gen. 18:12). Likewise, King David, though given Abishag to warm his bed in old age, was evidently impotent; the king "did not know her," says the Bible discreetly (1 Kings 1:1–4). On the other hand, old man Lot was truly admirable because in extreme old age, dead drunk, he still managed to impregnate his two concerned daughters (Gen. 19:30–38). Obviously sex is crucial in Israel. If the covenant promise—children as many as the stars in the sky and as the sand in the sea[9]—is to be fulfilled, sexual desire must lead to impregnation. Thus sex and commitment to covenant faith are intimately bound together.[10] The legendary heroes of Israel are often sexually active into old age, but they are unusual. For the most part, the elderly experience a waning of their sexual desires. So to sum it all up, old age in Israel seemed to begin earlier than in our more modern world, but, nevertheless, was much the same; we hear less, see less, taste less, and find less delight in sex. We grow old—it's the usual thing.

## "Honor Your Father and Mother"

So what does the Bible teach us about old age? We must begin with the Hebrew scriptures because, as we shall see, the Christian scriptures have little to say on the subject. So what does the Hebrew Bible tell us about old people?

At the outset, all societies in the ancient Middle East encourage esteem for the elderly. Basically, the elderly are to be respected, indeed honored for their wisdom, and children are to defer to their parents' gray-haired experience. Not only did societies urge respect for the elderly, they backed up their advice with law. For example, the Mesopotamian Code of Hammurabi provides terrible penalties for those who abuse parents; for example, "If a son has struck his father, they shall cut off his hand."[11] Israel embraced similar concerns although, surprisingly, Israel lists mothers as well as fathers in the laws. The Covenant Code in Ex. 20:22–23:33 classifies parent abuse as a capital offense: "Whoever strikes father or mother shall be put to death" (21:15), and "Whoever curses father or mother [implying some sort of systematic neglect] shall be put to death" (21:17).[12] In Deuteronomy, there are curses, one of which refers to those who degrade parents: "Cursed be anyone who dishonors father or mother" (Deut. 27:16). Again, in Deut. 21:18–21, a "stubborn and rebellious" son who will not obey parents can be brought before the elders of the community and, if deemed incorrigible ("a glutton and a drunkard"), then all the men of the village may stone him to death.[13] All these commandments are regarded as a binding word of the Lord. Listen:

> You shall rise before the aged [lit. gray head], and defer to the old,
> and you shall fear your God; I am the Lord. (Lev. 19:32)

So, adding it all up, respect for the elderly, indeed social provision for the elderly, was a part of Israel's covenant responsibility. Just as God was regarded as ancient and wise, "from everlasting to everlasting," so under God, those who are in old age are to be honored.[14]

But we must probe the matter more deeply. Why is the command to "honor your father and mother" so necessary? Many scholars suppose that the first three commandments guard God's holiness—you shall have no other gods, shall make no idols, and shall not take the Lord's name in vain.

Then commandments four and five are at a second level of high concern—keep the Sabbath and honor parents—after which come all the others in a rather more general way.[15] So why is honoring parents so important? Isn't such a commandment insensitive to the "Mommy Dearest" problems that children have with careless and often malicious parents? There are always tensions between parents and children, profound psychological tensions, that would seem to question any blind obedience to parental commands or any sweeping demand that we *must* honor our parents. For how can any son or daughter fully honor a parent who may be unjust or even petulant? Years ago we did clinical work with a patient who ended up in a mental institution because he was repeatedly punished by sadistic parents who slammed his genitals in a screen door; was he supposed to honor his father and mother? The fifth command does seem altogether too sweeping, particularly when backed up by capital punishment.

## Honor as Social Security

Of course, at the outset, we should recognize that the commandment is addressed to adult children. We are not to shout the command at little children or threaten them with stoning if they don't conform. "Honor your father and mother" is a social injunction designed for mature children and their even more mature parents. Moreover, the commandment addresses corporate Israel.[16] We Americans tend to read our Bibles as if every "you" were second-person singular. But the Fifth Commandment is addressed to Israel and is intended to define social policy. In other words, the commandment has more to do with social security issues than with psychological attitudes within the family. Just as the Sabbath day command may have been prompted by a concern for workers who need to have rest,[17] so the parental command provides respect and security for the aging. Though there may well be rancorous old people, selfish and impossible "gray heads," nonetheless the social order must find ways to support them compassionately. So we have a commandment: "Honor your father and your mother."

Still more deeply, the commandment addresses the progression of human beings across the sweep of time, generation after generation. My grandparents were served by my parents, and my parents served by me, and, in turn, I may be served by my children, and they in their time by their children. Our parents may have been wicked, almost as wicked as we are with our children, but, nonetheless, they are our parents and they have given us birth before God. The fact is that our aging parents will soon be replaced by aging us. Even as we may hope for patience and affection in our gray-headed years, so we seek to honor our father and mother. The commandment displays a kind of tenderness toward our common time-swept humanity. In so doing it calls for a certain civility between the generations, and not only civility but mercy. Good heavens, we are *all* bad parents, no matter how many courses in parenting we digest; we are *all* without exception sin-struck parents who damage our children. So, as sinners, who are the children of sinners, and who in turn breed sinners, we cling to the shape of human courtesy which, in a way, is the next best thing to love. We honor our fathers and our mothers and hope that our days will be long in the land God has given us.

## Is Old Age Wise?

Stop now and ask, Why should the elderly be revered? What is so special about old folk in the Bible? In the Bible, a long life is often viewed as a reward to the righteous and a sure sign of God's favor. Because, in general, the Hebrew scriptures expect no afterlife, moral rewards happen here and now; God rewards virtue by extending our years. So if people live to a ripe old age, have strength of body and mind, are respected, comfortably well-off, surrounded by children and grandchildren, then surely they have been blessed by God. David is described as dying "in a good old age, full of days, riches, and honor" (1 Chron. 29:28). Why? Because, according to First Chronicles, he sought to serve God with a "single mind and willing heart" and was rewarded by God who "searches every mind" (1 Chron. 28:9). In other words, the elderly deserve special respect because they are elderly and, if elderly, then obviously, they are people who have earned God's favor. Of course, the formula—many years equals the favor of God—doesn't always follow. Job raises the blunt question: "Why do the wicked live on, reach old age, and grow mighty in power? . . . They spend their days in prosperity, and in peace they go down to Sheol" (Job 21:7, 13). Yes, wicked and rancorous old people may live long lives, but, as a general rule, the Bible seems to suppose that God gives many days to the righteous. And Job himself, a virtuous man, is certainly rewarded for his fidelity, with thousands of farm animals, as well as children to the fourth generation. "Job died old," says the Bible with admiration, "and full of days." The elderly are those whose virtues have been rewarded by a gift of time and, surely, their virtue deserves our honor.

What about the shibboleth that the aged are wise? Yes, the Bible does speak of the wisdom of the elderly, and, in fact, before the monarchy Israel was basically ruled by tribal "elders." What's more, the idea that the elderly can instruct us fills wisdom literature:[18]

> The fear of the LORD is the beginning of knowledge;
>     fools despise wisdom and instruction.
> Hear, my child, your father's instruction,

and do not reject your mother's teaching;
for they are a fair garland for your head,
and pendants for your neck.
(Prov. 1:7–9)

But the shadow of senile confusion hangs over us all;[19] are old people automatically wise? In the Bible, they are not. Think of Isaac who becomes so muddled that he blesses the wrong son and doesn't know the difference. Or remember the priest Eli and old King Saul, both of whom end up confused and incapable of continuing leadership. Likewise, King David loses more than a step as he ages; he can no longer handle the intrigues of his own court. No, the wisdom that the elderly possess would seem to be not so much intellectual quickness as a kind of practical wisdom shaped by experience. There was an old farmer in northern Michigan who seemed to know how to do everything. "There's a leak in the barn, Godfrey, what do we do?" Usually, he wouldn't answer; he'd merely say, "Come on." He'd walk you into his workshop, cut lids from a tin can, slice the side of the can and unroll it, hammering it flat. Then he would hand you the flat metal to shove under a shingle and stop the leak. Obviously, he had jammed tin cans up under shingles many times before. He was smart by right of experience. So in the Bible the elderly have practical wisdom and, incidentally, a practical moral wisdom as well—right-and-wrong wisdom that only a fool would ignore. So the aged possess well-aged wisdom.

But more, the elderly have been given a particular perspective. They regard life quite differently than do the young. For the elderly have begun to number their days; they know that soon they will not be. The apocalyptic book *Testaments of the Twelve Patriarchs,* from the second century before Christ, is a huge collection of deathbed wisdom supposedly from the twelve sons of Jacob. They review their lives, confess their sins, and exhort virtue. They also gaze into an envisioned future. Such a book demonstrates the real wisdom of the old, wisdom instructed by a kind of hard realism; old folk know they will soon die. So, for them, each day is bright with light no matter how hampered they may be—along with Dylan Thomas, they are willing to "rage, rage against the dying of the light" and, therefore, to bless most youthful pleasures.[20] There can be a sweet moral freedom in the elderly, because they may have learned what does and doesn't matter.[21] But they have also begun to ask what meaning there may be to the succeeding generations and, therefore, to have some vision of God's good purposes. Perhaps the aged have learned to cling to the grand promises of God, a God who alone is everlasting. Yes, a surface mental confusion may strike down the elderly, but where there is a brooding force of mind there can be a kind of wisdom often unavailable elsewhere, a wisdom that begins with the words of Psalm 90: "Teach us to count our days" (v. 12).[22]

## Old Age in the Gospels

Turning now to the Christian scriptures, we ask, What do the Christian scriptures add to our understanding? The blunt answer: Not much! Jesus doesn't seem to address the issue of elderly care. In fact, Jesus is abrupt on the subject of family responsibility. When his mother comes to chase him down, he doesn't even bother to talk to her—"Here," he says, pointing to a crowd around him, "here are my mother and my brothers!" (Mark 3:31–35). And doesn't Matthew (10:35) picture Jesus quoting the prophet Micah, and saying, "I have come to set a man against his father, and a daughter against her mother, and a daughter-in-law against her mother-in-law"? Then, to cap it all, there is a harsh logion from the Q source: "Whoever comes to me and does not hate father and mother . . . cannot be my disciple" (Luke 14:26). Jesus' words are scarcely fit to scribble on a Mother's Day card! What on earth is going on here? Well, such teachings made sense in the radical situation in which the Christian movement began. Apparently disciples had left their families to follow Jesus. Subsequently, they were probably read out of their families for being a part of sectarian Christianity. Sociologically speaking, wandering charismatic preachers are not what you'd call good candidates for Christian Family Life awards![23] The teachings of Jesus that contradict the whole idea of honoring parents may have some actual historical basis.

But dare we ask about a deeper alienation? Jesus preached the coming of a new social order, what he termed the "kingdom of God." Evidently his message quickened opposition among Sadducees, Pharisees, Herodians, and a group mentioned simply as "the Elders." Would the prophetic announcement of God's new order trigger opposition from people in power, people who in Israel were largely older—older priests, Sadducees, Pharisees, and community leaders? Are they representatives of the "old wine" and the "old garments" that Jesus has come to replace? Does such real tension underlie the so-called "antitheses" in Matthew 5: "You have heard that it was said to those of ancient times . . . but I say to you"? Yes, the phrase may be a rabbinic formula, saying in effect, "Now I will give you the true meaning of the ancient wisdom," but nevertheless there is a rhetorical tension between the "it was said" and the "I say to you."[24] Was the early Christian movement to some extent a youth rebellion? Perhaps. For with few exceptions, the teaching of Jesus does not mention the elderly. Even his most famous parable, the Prodigal Son, as Bernard Brandon Scott observes, depicts a father who astonishingly gives in to a disrespectful younger son, who fails to demand due honor, and who in the end seems to give up his status as a respected senior citizen.[25] But make no mistake, Jesus upheld the law of God: When the rich young ruler asked for guidance, Jesus cited the commandments, including "Honor your father and mother" (Mark 10:19). And certainly he condemned Pharisees who, by chicanery, could disclaim financial responsibility for their parents:

> Then he said to them, "You have a fine way of rejecting the commandment of God in order to keep your tradition! For Moses said, 'Honor your father and your mother'; and 'Whoever speaks evil of father or mother must surely die.' But you say that if anyone tells father or mother, 'Whatever support you might have had from me is Corban' (that is, an offering to God)—then you no longer permit doing anything for a father or mother, thus making void the word of God through your tradition that you have handed on. And you do many things like this." (Mark 7:9–13)

So what can we make of the Gospels? Jesus seems to uphold family responsibility and yet at the same time denies binding family ties for himself and his disciples? Perhaps he is setting family loyalties within the horizon of God's new order in which all our conventional social patterns may be completely passé. If a kingdom of God is imminent, then are normal social conventions somewhat irrelevant? Perhaps.

Maybe there's still another explanation. For Christians, is the nuclear family being replaced by a community of faith? Maybe for Christians blood is *not* "thicker than water," that is, the water of baptism. Is Christian community intended to replace conventions of the family? Perhaps. Surely, in the Gospel of John, when Jesus turns over his mother to the "beloved disciple," saying, "Woman, here is your son," and to the disciple, "Here is your mother," is he not appealing to such an understanding? For early Christian people, the church was clearly a true family, a truer family than their own previous blood relationships. Incidentally, in faith, Christian communities may still provide a closer-than-family support to members. Christianity rightly understood may put our family in the Lord ahead of our genetic families.[26] Maybe we are to be family members of the new humanity before anything else. Maybe.

The Pauline letters offer no more support for family customs than do the Gospel records, perhaps less. Yes, Paul deals with issues relating to family tensions. But in Paul's thought we find the same pejorative use of the word "old," as in "old leaven," "old self," and "old ways." Rather obviously, Paul's apocalyptic vision of time is involved; he views time as divided into "the present age" and an "age to come." With the resurrection, the present age is passing away and a new age has been initiated under the rule of Christ. So if the new creation has begun, then "new" is a positive term, and the "old" is passing away.

## Christianity and the Family

Later Christian literature becomes much more conventional. By then there are Christian families and thus Christian old folk to be honored. So in Luke-Acts we get a repeated call to care for the widows and for the handicapped. Moreover we get types of elderly leadership showing up—Elizabeth and Zechariah, Simeon and Anna. Later, the pastoral epistles—First and Second Timothy and Titus—demonstrate respect for elderly leadership as do the general epistles, such as First Peter, which evidently was written by an "elder." Of course, the book of Revelation pictures Messiah as having hair of wool and, later, describes twenty-four elders surrounding the throne of God. Later Christian literature seems to return to the traditions of Israel.

But there is an interesting change. Roman society was dominated by the notion of *patria potestas*, in which a father has unlimited power over offspring. So, though later epistles do urge children to honor parents with obedience, they introduce a certain moderation, if not give-and-take, to relationships. For example, in the epistles we find *Haustafeln*, household codes of behavior, to guide family living (Col. 3:20–21; Eph. 6:1–4).[27] The lists add "mother" along with "father," but, above all, they restrict *patria potestas* in love and, rightly, set both parents and children "in the Lord."

> Children, obey your parents in the Lord, for this is right. "Honor your father and mother"—this is the first commandment with a promise: "so that it may be well with you and you may live long on the earth."
>
> And, fathers, do not provoke your children to anger, but bring them up in the discipline and instruction of the Lord. (Eph. 6:1–4)

Already, life in the new order of God is beginning to shape family life.

## Old Age and Us

So here we are, Americans in the 1990s. Our situation is suddenly complicated. Could the Bible envision Maggie Kuhn and the Gray Panthers? And what of so-called entitlement programs—Social Security and Medicare—that are now rising to consume a huge chunk of the national budget? Deeper still, during the Reagan years, obviously the rich got richer while the poor multiplied.[28] Now our children and our children's children may be expected to be worse off than the current parental generation. Will resentments bristle? All you have to do is to review Solomon's reign, in which the old leaders were pushed aside by an aggressive younger generation.[29] The fact is, American policy toward the elderly is currently up for grabs. Is white America adding "ageism" to already evident "racism" and "sexism"?

What on earth does an antique book, the Bible, have to say to our generation? Simply put: the Bible urges social legislation for the elderly. As a nation, we are to honor our parents, as well as those who provide for their care. More, we must find ways for aged wisdom of older citizens to instruct us. Let's not talk about giving oldsters self-esteem; self-esteem is not really a Christian concept. No, let us truly esteem a wisdom of age that can serve us all. And, along with the elderly, let us stand before the mystery of dying and, thereby, see into the mysteries of living. Someday, sings the prophet Joel, when God pours out Holy Spirit on us all, "your old people shall dream dreams, and your young shall see visions" (Joel 2:28, modified). The two phrases are not disconnected—old dreams are the thread from which young visions are woven.

There is a fine final vision to be found in the Bible; it shows up in the words of the prophet Zechariah. Zechariah pictures Jerusalem when the Lord God returns to Zion. He sees a good society in God's future where young and old will live together in shared joy. Listen, for the prophet's words depict everything we want for generations together:

> Thus spoke the Lord of Hosts: Old men and old women will again sit in the parks of Jerusalem, each with a staff in hand, because of great age. And the parks of the city will be filled with boys and girls playing. (Zech. 8:4–5)[30]

The description is poignant: Here are old folk sitting in the sun, propped up by canes, while boys and girls race around playing together. Yet there's a sense of something altogether fitting about the vision. In the Bible, whatever is fitting, is usually good!

**SERMON**

# Before the Stars Go Dark

David G. Buttrick

*Occasion for sermon:* The sermon was preached in the Sharp Chapel of the University of Tulsa at a conference on ministry to the aging sponsored by Phillips Theological Seminary. Following David Buttrick's usual practice, the sermon was untitled, and his translation of Eccl. 11:7–12:8, 13 was read, as follows:

> 11:7 Light is sweet; it's a pleasure for eyes to see the sunshine.
> 8 So anyone who lives many years should enjoy them all; but re-

member the days of darkness, for they will be many. Everything that comes along is vanity.[1]

9 Be happy, young person, while you are young, and revel in the days of your prime. Follow the impulses of your heart and the desires of your eyes, [but know that God will bring you to judgment for all these things].[2] 10 Drive cares from your heart, and put pain from your body; for youth and dark hair are fleeting. 12:1 So remember your grave in the days of your youth,[3] before days of trouble come, and the years near when you will say,
"I have no pleasure in them."
2 Before the sun and the light—the moon and the stars—are darkened,
   and the clouds return after rain;
3 In the day when the guards of the house tremble,
   and the strong men are bent,
 and the women grinding cease for they are few,
   and those who look through windows see dimly;
4 when the doors to the street will be shut,
   and the sound of the mill becomes still,
And one wakes up at the sound of a bird,
   and all the daughters of song are brought low;
5 when one is afraid of heights,
   and terrors lie in the roadway;
And the almond tree blossoms white,
   the grasshopper drags itself along,
   and the aphrodisiacs fail;[4]
For human beings must go to their long-lasting home,
   and the mourners will wander the streets;
6 Before the silver chord is snapped,
   and the golden bowl is shattered,
 and the pitcher lies broken by the fountain,
   and the wheel is smashed at the cistern,
7 And dust returns to the earth as it was,
   and life-breath goes back to God who gave it.
8 Vanity of vanities, says Qoheleth;
   everything is vanity. . . .
13 Now that all has been heard, in conclusion: Fear God and keep the commandments, for such is the whole duty of humankind.

There's a coffee-table picture book about aging. The pictures are remarkable. For on every open pagespread, there are two pictures: one of a young person and the other of the same person grown old. The young pictures are alive, smooth-skinned, and bright-eyed; they are beautiful. But then so are the old faces, faces that seem to have weathered into portraits of themselves. A blurb on the back of the book says that the photographer has "captured the mystery of aging." Well, the word is right; growing old is mysterious. Listen, for Ecclesiastes has turned the mystery of aging into poetry: "We wake with the sound of a bird; and all the daughters of song are brought low . . . [when] the almond tree blossoms white." Let us consider the mystery of aging.

# I

Well, Ecclesiastes may be poetry, but the poetry is full of realism. Hard realism. Ecclesiastes sees what happens to old people with wide-eyed honesty. Like an old house, human beings get run down—strong backs are bent, bright eyes dim, we begin to be afraid of falling down or of stumbling in pathways, our hair turns white, we shuffle our feet along, and sex, well, sex can be such a struggle. Listen, it's all very well to wave our coffee mugs with "Carpe diem"—"Seize the day"—scribbled on them, but how do we seize the waning hours of a long late afternoon? Well, bravado fades! A few years ago, a wealthy woman checked into a New York nursing home. Her chauffeur moved in a chaise lounge, a portable bar, a VCR for the movies, a big-screen TV, and a rare oriental tapestry to hide the door out into the hall. She even hired a full-time maid. "You've got all the comforts of home," a nurse observed. "But I'm still old," the lady snarled. No matter how comfortable, no matter how well-provided for age can be, the Bible knows the truth. "The almond tree blossoms white, the grasshopper drags along, and the aphrodisiacs fail." The aging process goes one way: The fact is, we all get old.

What's worse, inevitably we begin to number our days. We start calculating the years we may have left. If you are sixty-five, well, you can't help noticing that the median life span is seventy-five. Oh, nowadays if you make it to sixty-five, you can usually figure on fifteen years more. But, ten or ten plus five, you still can count the years on your fingertips! You know that someday friends will look on your desk and find an unfinished letter you were going to write or maybe a date book with appointments you were going to keep. Perhaps they'll spot a pair of shoes beside your bed that you were planning to put on in the morning. Will there be a book dog-eared to mark the last page you read? "The pitcher lies broken by the fountain, the wheel is smashed at the cistern, and dust returns to the earth." Oh, most old folk have come to terms with dying. Ludwig Bemelmans tells of a prim English governess who worked for a world traveler; she had a casket shipped ahead wherever she went because, according to Bemelmans, "she didn't want to be caught short."[5] She was a realist. Old people do not torment themselves with dying, and yet, somewhere along the line, they do begin to number their days: "Before the silver cord is snapped and the golden bowl is shattered . . . and dust returns to the earth." When you're old you count the years.

Of course, the problem with having to die is not death so much as judgment. Sooner or later, we are forced to face up to our lives. "God will bring you to judgment," says Qoheleth, matter-of-factly. Look, we're not talking about Jesus Christ perched on a throne in some golden-streeted, pearl-gated, beclouded city of heavenly hereafter. No, Christian faith is not a nursery rhyme! But if we believe in God, a moral God, then somehow, somewhere there's going to be a weighing of our lives. Maybe judgment will be nothing more than a dream of tears in God's eyes and a terrible sense of "Oh God, what haven't I done." We are not talking about great big sins—most Christians don't have imagination enough for great big sins. No, the deep regrets we have are over our general failure to be saintly. We should have given ourselves away extravagantly. We should have loved and loved and loved, freely and with such frisky good humor that we transformed every neighbor into family. We should have fed the hungry at our own table and clothed the ragged with our own clothes. We should . . . We should . . . So a modern poet, sitting in a subway train tunneling under city streets, overhears inadvertent confessions of greed and indifference all around him. He realizes that all his life, he has "always, at all times, been a willing accomplice." Suddenly he is swept by a sense of guilt. "I am guilty of what? Of guilt. Guilty of guilt," he thinks, "that is all, and enough."[6] The problem isn't death; no, it's a sense of our own too-late, mislived lives.

## II

So how do you live growing old? Qoheleth has some good advice. *When you are young, you enjoy your life.* For Qoheleth knows that God created a whole wide world and named it "Good. Very good!" God has given us pleasure. So we can play games together and party and be exhilarated in our own young flesh; why not? If you are given a gift, surely you are supposed to unwrap it! Wasn't it Bernard Shaw who claimed that "youth is wasted on the young?" Maybe. So, finally, the aging have figured out how to enjoy life—each bright day, a gift unwrapped—but unfortunately they may be frail. Remember the girl Emily in Thornton Wilder's *Our Town*. She's dead but, by some magic, she is allowed to return invisible and take a look at life one last time. She revels in the ordinary: in ticking clocks, sunflowers, the smell of a freshly ironed dress, the taste of coffee, food, sleeping, waking up. She realizes that the sweet earth is too wondrous for anyone to grasp.[7] How do we live? We take our cue from Emily Gibbs; we try to realize life while we live. Like wide-eyed children, we can delight in life, have giggling delight with no holding back. "Be happy, young people, when you are young. Revel in your youth," says old Qoheleth. But he missed the point. We can revel in old age as well, for everyday the "light is sweet."

Well, is there more? Yes. Qoheleth adds a final word. "In conclusion," he says, "fear God and keep the commandments." There is in each of us a kind of good little child meekness that can bow before God and say, "Your will be done." Oh, we are not meant to wander through life memorizing all the laws that are listed in the Bible, like tourists with a guidebook who foolishly read their way through the wonders of Europe. No, in spite of Presbyterians who may suppose so, the Christian life is not slavish obedience. But look, it isn't a vague religiousness either—a warm-tub Jesus feeling in the heart. We know that God wants us to live as sisters and brothers, which means that we stand up and outright disavow racism and sexism and, yes, our homophobic reactions—both in the military and in our churches. We know that God wants peace on earth, so yes, we will support an army in hungry Somalia, but no, in the midst of all the flag-waving, we will condemn the slaughter of an unjust Gulf War. All our days, we must live with an end-term vision of what God wants for the human world and then passionately seek to do God's commandments—commandments that are, after all, woven out of a vision of God's good pupose. Everything has been heard, says Qoheleth: "In conclusion," he says, "fear God and keep the commandments."

Well, is there anything else? Is there anything more to be said about growing old? We are to enjoy life while we live, fear God, and keep the commandments. Is there anything else that matters? No. Anything else is vanity—all vanity.

# 4

# The Biblical Age:
# Images of Aging and the Elderly

*Jon L. Berquist*

In our modern society, it is common to think of the aging process as fixed. Even though age affects everyone differently, it still affects everyone. The pattern of growth, maturation, and age seems certain; this pattern is the basis of developmental theories that inform our sense of self, our strategies for life choices and child rearing, and even the structure of education, with grade levels based on age.[1] We notice individual variation, but usually we do not notice the differences between cultures.[2] This raises the first problem in investigating the Bible's attitudes about aging. Ancient Israel and early Christianity present the interpreter with cultures that are profoundly different from those we know today.

Many of the changes are quite recent. Today, we think of life spans in the United States as about seventy-five or eighty years, on average. As recently as the 1880s, however, children born in the United States could only expect a life of less than forty-five years.[3] In just over a century, life spans have almost doubled, reaching levels before unknown in human history. This adds to our interpretative difficulties, since our lives are so different from those of our ancestors.

The first task, therefore, is an examination of aging in ancient Israel and the world of early Christianity. From that base, we can proceed to investigate the Bible's attitudes about society's oldest members and about the process of aging itself. Then we can focus on a series of specific texts that discuss aging and the elderly, searching for insights into the appropriation of these stories and values for our own situations in today's world.

Aging represents at least two separate concepts: the process of physical and social maturation and change throughout the life span, and the social perceptions and definitions of the roles and expectations for those whom the society defines as elderly. The first issue places aging within a larger discussion of the entire maturation process, involving the whole life span.

That larger framework provides the proper context for understanding ancient Israel's social perceptions of the elderly.

## The Life Cycle
## in Ancient Israel

During the years of early Israel (1300–1000 B.C.E.), the time before the rise of the monarchy in Jerusalem, life was extremely difficult for the Israelites. They lived a hand-to-mouth existence in the rough hill country around the Canaanite cities. Each member of the community struggled to provide enough food to eat. The whole village might have a small flock of goats, sheep, or other small animals. Those members charged with herding this flock might be away from the village for long periods while searching for adequate pasture land for the animals. Because the rains were sporadic at best in early Israel, the flock might have to travel long distances to find enough wild grass to survive. Closer to the village, other members of the community would do some small-scale farming, probably concentrating on crops of grain. Many of the villagers would forage for small game and also nuts and berries. Collecting and producing food required the efforts of the whole community, from the youngest to the oldest, just to have enough food for survival.[4]

This different lifestyle required huge amounts of cooperative labor from everyone to ensure the survival of the community as well as of each individual. The labor itself was backbreaking; it took a substantial toll on each person within early Israel. As a result, their life cycle was much different from those we expect today in industrial North America. The most frequent causes of death in early Israel would have been accident, plague, and starvation, especially for men. For women, the leading cause of death was complications arising from pregnancy and childbirth.[5] Under these conditions, ancient societies such as urban Greece had life expectancies that were very short by today's standards. Some scholars have argued for life spans of twenty-five to thirty years.[6] The data for ancient Israel's rural areas are probably even more sobering. Adulthood came much earlier for these early Israelites, and causes of death such as accident, infection, and childbirth affected them much earlier in the life cycle than middle-class industrial North Americans are affected. The rates of death were so high that the society needed a very high birthrate in order to survive, but this created a problem, since childbirth was a leading cause of death. It was essential for couples to bear children as soon as possible, before some accident or plague brought death and ended the possibility for reproduction. Thus, early Israelite couples may have procreated at ages as young as fourteen. If health and circumstances allowed, Israelite women would begin a new pregnancy approximately every three years. Many of these births would result in children who would not live to see their first birthday, because the infant mortality rates were so high. A greater danger was the risk of complications at the birth itself. Under these conditions, many women died before they reached the age of twenty. Without the physical dangers of childbirth, men would have lived longer, but their increased exposure to intertribal warfare as well as accidents in hunting may have made it rare for men to live past the age of twenty-five.[7]

If a man's life expectancy was twenty-five and a woman's was twenty years, then life for early Israelites was much different from life for most modern people. In order to have a high enough percentage of the populace involved in producing food, children as young as ages four or five would need to share some of the tasks. About a quarter of one's life would be spent married. In many cases, a fourteen-year-old man would marry a fourteen-year-old woman, who would die in childbirth when they were both twenty. The man might then marry a fifteen-year-old woman, and they would have another set of children before they both died five years later. This might leave two or three or four children as orphans, raised by relatives. Some of the children would never have known their parents, but would only know the village who raised them. Almost no one would know grandparents.

## Age in the Cities

As Israel developed into a monarchy, the conditions of life changed, at least for some of the people.[8] Life in the cities was much easier; city dwellers basked in much greater wealth than people in the surrounding countryside. City people often owned farmland out in the valleys and collected rent on that productive soil, or they worked as merchants or craftspersons. These city occupations were much less risky than rural occupations, and so the city dwellers faced much lower death rates from accidents.[9] Also, since the city folk were richer, they purchased better food. Whereas rural people would have eaten mostly berries, tubers, and grains, the urbanites would have had a wider range of choices: along with the grains, dairy products, meat, and some fruits, perhaps even including some imported delicacies such as nuts. A greater mix of nutrients and a higher calorie level, plus a higher amount of protein, may have significantly extended life expectancies.

Throughout the period of the monarchy, wealthy persons may have lived to ages such as fifty, sixty, or even seventy. But attaining such ages would have been statistically rare within Israelite society, since these wealthy city dwellers accounted for a small percentage of the Israelite population. (Even societies such as ancient Greece after the period of Israel's monarchy may have had life expectancies of about thirty-five years for women and forty-five years for men.[10]) According to 2 Sam. 5:5, David lived to be seventy. In rare cases, some people may have lived to the age of eighty.

Age, then, was a relative thing in early and monarchic Israel. In the vastly complicated social situation, city folk lived much longer lives than their rural relatives—roughly three times as long.[11] This gulf of experience and expectation affected Israel's social existence in numerous ways, and the society's perceptions of age were chief among these.

## Age in the Villages

For villagers, what we know as old age would have been a rare commodity. Their rural culture involved such hard living that the age of twenty would have begun one's elder years, and one would reach surprisingly advanced age sometime in the mid-twenties. But in certain circumstances, people did live longer, and those people would have received special notice within the community. Some men would survive accidents and attain better health than others; if they also lived in a time and a region of peace, they might live into their thirties. Such men would be village elders for years, and they would even live long enough to see their children grow into the adulthood of their late teen years. Certain women as well would survive the dangers of childbirth and live into their late twenties and early thirties. The village's barren women might live longer by avoiding their society's chief cause of death. These men and women would form a valuable resource for the village, because their great accumulation of knowledge could offer a community significant advantages. Such respected elders operated as a community's institutional memory, having lived through many more life situations than the younger members, and thus they could share insights and analogies to teach the next generation about the world and to help the village make important decisions.[12] Though these elders were older and more experienced than the other villagers, they could hardly be considered "aged" by modern standards; perhaps they were as old as thirty, and they would still be as strong and healthy as anyone else in the community, barring injury. Their relatively advanced age resulted from random avoidance of accidents or safe survival of childbirth more than any other factors.

## What Age Means:
## Israelite Perceptions of Age

If most villagers died in their twenties, they must have regarded the city dwellers with awe. Some inhabitants of cities such as Jerusalem might have lived two or three times as long, because of better nutrition and lower occupational hazards. The gap was amazing. As an extreme example, a king might live to be seventy, as David did. Even though half of the villagers would have no memory of parents, and hardly any would have known grandparents, the king might remember a young villager's great-grandparents or even farther back. Approaching the king would have brought a villager into the presence of a being who knew things that would have been otherwise unknowable, even by local village elders or family tradition. The villagers might have seen the cities as magical places, full of people who (almost) never die.[13] The average inhabitant of Jerusalem, for instance, would have been older than any but the oldest of the villagers.[14] Thus, for the villagers, "old" might have characterized certain individuals within their own communities, but "elderly" would have been nearly synonymous with "city dweller."[15]

Within the cities themselves, however, age would have a different meaning. If the average life span (at least for men) was around sixty or seventy, then a person would reach the middle years of life during the thirties and forties, and the physiological changes of aging might begin in the fifties and continue through the sixties. Although this pattern of aging is still substantially younger than that of modern middle-class North Americans, it is at least more familiar to most of us than the experience of the early Israelite villagers, for whom old age meant the age of twenty. But the city dwellers still faced an existence far different from that of most modern North Americans. If their life span was longer than their rural relatives', their average age of marriage was probably not much greater, and women's most frequent cause of death was still childbirth. This meant that a man might outlive his first wife by up to fifty years. If that man kept remarrying, even if he never had more than one wife at a time, he could still have many wives. Such a man would live to see the children of these marriages, as well as grandchildren from his earlier unions and, in some cases, even great-grandchildren.[16]

The added financial resources of most city dwellers offered men another option—more than one wife at a time. Very few of the nomadic Israelites of biblical stories (such as the characters of the books of Genesis and Exodus) had many wives, but many urban Israelites (and especially the wealthy ones, such as the royal family) had several wives, and a few would have had dozens.

Old age, then, was typically limited to the city's men; much less frequently did women experience advanced age. Since the city valued the expertise and knowledge gained through age and the resultant years of exposure to life, city life radically increased the value given to men in the society. The elders who sat at the gate to share their wisdom with the community and to make governmental and legal decisions for the city would have been almost exclusively male. The value placed on years of experience biased the society toward the men.[17] Patriarchy is the rule of the fathers, and as such, patriarchy consisted of more than the privileging of males; it also assumed the privileging of age. In ancient Israel, these two factors in social privilege were highly correlated. Together, they formed a certain dominance for the male elders of the community. The respect for the elderly in ancient Israel, often cited as an aspect of Old Testament thought to be emulated today in resistance to the youth culture, in reality reflects a preference for a male group of older elites, who were present almost exclusively in the cities among the wealthy. These top elites had a distinctive lifestyle and set of social roles and expectations, reflecting their social esteem and privilege.

## The Roles of the Elderly

Israel's only true elderly, therefore, would primarily be the urban men, and the group considered "elders" might include those wealthy, powerful urban men over the age of fifty. They would be significantly older than anyone outside the cities, and they would have already outlived many of their colleagues. These elders would have served their military time, but they would still (as a group) be in fine physical health. Their power and prestige, in both economic and governmental arenas, would be unstoppable. These city elders had several important roles within the community that went beyond their material roles as elites. They were already persons of economic and political power, but their role as elders gave them a strong sense of wisdom. They were knowledgeable, because of their additional years of experience, and they were connected, because they had built larger networks of friends and acquaintances over the years.[18] These were the elders of Israel, the truly powerful group of controlling men (and some women).[19]

Within both the villages and the cities, the elderly exercised great control. The Pentateuchal stories, especially those of the exodus and wilderness narratives, are filled with references to the elders of the community. In Hebrew, there is no separate word for "elder" or "elderly"—both concepts are present in the word for an older person. Leaders such as Moses—himself an elderly man—operated within the context of a group of elderly persons who shared power and influence. Israelite society was a gerontocracy—a rule by the elderly, for the elderly—with few exceptions, such as the upstart reign of that boyish figure David. This is the case throughout the stories of ancient Israel. When David's son Absalom revolts, there is a certain power within his youthful energy, but much of the story revolves around the conflicting advice given to David and Absalom by their aged counselors. In earlier stories, such as Numbers 11, the elders of the people and the officers of the people are equivalent terms. To be old is to be in a position of power. The elders make decisions for a city and represent it in legal disputes with other cities and other villages; they operate as a board of trustees with legal responsibility for the happenings of their community (Deuteronomy 21).

## Israel's Attitudes
## toward the Elderly

Old age, then, was equivalent to a position of great respect in ancient Israel. At several points, the Old Testament mentions graying hair as a sign of respect. Proverbs 16:31 offers the following perspective: "Gray hair is a crown of glory; it is gained in a righteous life."[20] Operative here are other Old Testament assumptions as well. God grants length of life to those who are particularly good or righteous, and so gray hair comes only to those who possess long life as a reward for their goodness in their younger days. Certainly, anyone who avoided the accidents and tragedies of ancient existence and survived the tumults of youthful dangers would have been thought to be blessed; only those specially chosen by God could enter the rarefied ages of the thirties and forties, and only a very select few would have lived to achieve graying hair.

Likewise, Prov. 20:29 comments that "the glory of youths is their strength, but the beauty of the aged is their gray hair." The proverbs typically stem from a later time in Israel's history, when advanced age was more common, and when persons would live not only long enough to become gray but long enough to lose some physical vitality. This wisdom writing urges that the contributions of the aging are not to be measured in their physical strength, for that is the proper contribution of younger folk. The elderly are measured differently, according to their own abilities. In ancient Israel, the power of the young resided in their bodies, but the power of the elderly was in their heads—not because of the grayness of the temple, but because of the wisdom and the networks contained therein, and the power that they wielded in the social arena.

The Old Testament also limits the power of the elderly, as it limits and rightly contextualizes all human power. Both young and old alike are subject to God's power, and that is always a power to save. Deutero-Isaiah offers the beautiful portrait of God's care for all:

> Listen to me, O house of Jacob, all the remnants of the house of Israel,
>      who have been borne by me from your birth, carried from your
>      womb;
> even to your old age, I am the one, even when you turn gray I will
>      carry you.
> I have made, I will bear; I will carry, I will save.

> (Isa. 46:3–4, author's translation)

God's care and compassion extend throughout all of human life; all ages receive God's protection and intervention equally, and there are no favorites. Both youth and age are valued by God, and God's presence and involvement radically limit the rights of either group to control the other.

Still, the Old Testament sees old age as a blessing from God, and thus a sign of proper living and of appropriate, well-deserved divine favor. Perhaps the best example is Job, that wealthy aristocrat and that poor, blighted soul. His numerous children die as a result of the wager between God and the Satan, but the story ends in a much different tenor. God restores to Job what was lost, though one must argue that new children never restore the loss caused by the death of any beloved child. God blessed Job's latter days more than his earlier days (Job 42:12), and this blessing can be measured. Job now possesses twice as many livestock as before, and he gains ten new children, long after the first ones are already grown and dead through tragedy. After the births of the ten, Job lives another 140 years. He was aged before, but he enjoys an extremely long life. The blessing of such a long life brings a specific enjoyment: he sees not only his children and his grandchildren, but also his great-grandchildren. That special pleasure is rare enough in our days of extended life spans, but it would have been magical and miraculous in Job's days.

One can easily see the fantasy and the longing behind a story such as Job's. It would have been an all-too-common experience for parents to lose their children to accidents and tragedies. When a single child from the household falls prey to a disease or an accident, it is bad enough, but a family losing all of its children would have been an unsurpassable tragedy, and it would have been more common than any would care to know. In the face of such tragedy, what hope could there ever be? From the later story of Ruth, we hear of Naomi's lament after the death of her sons. She is too old for another set of children, and so she calls herself bitter—her hope for a future disappears at the graves of her sons. But Job has hope. By the grace of God, death is not the end—there are more children awaiting, and one can begin again. Not only does Job experience the joy of children once more, but God grants him life long enough to see several generations, and that gift was very rare.

Of course, people often fear and denounce what they themselves cannot have. A frightening folktale concerns Elisha, the prophetic successor of Elijah. Whereas Elijah became transported directly into heaven on flaming chariots when he reached the end of his days, Elisha grew old in more normal, human fashion. Once, while he was on the road between cities, some young boys came out from one of the cities, and they laughed at him, saying, "Get out of here, you baldhead!" Elisha took this rather poorly, and called down two bears from the woods who mauled forty-two of the boys to death (2 Kings 2:23–25). Perhaps these rural boys were frightened because they so rarely saw an old person (and since old people were only in the city, there may well have been other reasons to fear their power); perhaps they thought that the loss of hair was magical or demonic. Perhaps these boys knew that their own fathers had died at ages much younger than Elisha, and they saw him as unnatural. The story speaks of youth's fear of the aging process and of the power of the elderly—and the story also demonstrates that power of elders in a forceful, violent way.

Although typically the Old Testament respects old age, it also expresses fear of it. Other texts, especially among the later books that the Roman and Orthodox churches call deutero-canonical and Protestants consider apocryphal, manifest a more balanced approach to the benefits of aging. Consider these meditations from Wisd. Sol. 4:7–9:

> But the righteous, though they die early, will be at rest.
> For old age is not honored for length of time, or measured by
>     number of years;
> but understanding is gray hair for anyone, and a blameless life is ripe
>     old age.

This text realizes that age is blessed but also that it is not the only value in life. Righteousness is of more value than age. Likewise, understanding is a greater blessing than gray hair, and deserves the greater respect among the community. Of course, any of these writers would have instantly recognized that age and wisdom usually go hand in hand, but the Wisdom of Solomon recognizes that there are exceptions. Age by itself is no blessing, though the usual effects of age, such as righteousness and understanding, are greatly to be valued and praised.

The book of Sirach offers a similar observation:

> If you gathered nothing in your youth,
>     how can you find anything in your old age?
> How attractive is sound judgment in the gray-haired,
>     and for the aged to possess good counsel!
> How attractive is wisdom in the aged,
>     and understanding and counsel in the venerable!
> Rich experience is the crown of the aged,
>     and their boast is the fear of the Lord.
> (Sirach 25:3–6)

Again, the wisdom and the experience of the elderly receive great praise, but these are not the ultimate virtues. Sirach offers the practical observation that one must gather experience and wisdom throughout one's life if one expects to have it in old age. The first gray hair does not bestow instant wisdom upon the fool any more than "wisdom teeth" indicate any true powers of mind or soul. Instead, these are indicators of age, and age offers the opportunity to gather the right kinds of experience to make life full—if one takes proper advantage of those opportunities as they present themselves.

The Old Testament perspective on aging and the elderly, therefore, is a very balanced one. Age is a rare commodity, and it offers great power and privilege within the community. Age also offers the ability to acquire experiences and to share them with others. Thus age and its attendant wisdom carry the responsibility to care for the community. Of course, age itself is not enough; one must have acquired wisdom and integrity along with it in order to best serve the community in one's old age, whenever that occurs.

## The Differences in
## the New Testament Situation

Sirach is a text from the period between ancient Israel and the world of the New Testament. Texts such as this show a tempering of ancient Israel's picture of age. Gray hair is not the only sign needed to be considered valuable; one must also demonstrate wisdom. Gathering experiences is not as important as comprehending experience so that one can apply it for a better life. By the time of the New Testament writings, there is a further shift in the perceptions of age.

In the Hellenistic and Roman world, the economic conditions had improved to the extent that more people lived comfortable lives. There were more cities with more people who lived longer.[21] Perhaps even the peasants had better food and safer conditions than in previous centuries, and so even they lived a little longer. Of course, slaves still suffered dangerous living conditions and minimal nutrition, which shortened their life spans. But overall there was a greater life expectancy, and thus a pattern of life more near the modern middle-class expectation.

Correspondingly, the New Testament knows several elderly people, such as Elizabeth and Zechariah (Luke 1:5–25). Jesus' parables express no surprise at men who live to see two grown children (Luke 15:11–32). Still, people took note when Peter and John healed a man who was more than forty years old (Acts 4:22). His healing was remarkable because the conventional wisdom of that day insisted that people that old do not see their health improve. First Timothy 5:9 defines a social service to care for widows over sixty; younger ones should take care of themselves. A fifty-year-old is not too old, in New Testament times. These numbers provide a context for thinking about age in the urban New Testament communities. A forty-year-old is past middle age, in a period of life when one expects health to decline. Perhaps people in their late forties and early fifties were like today's groups of younger "senior citizens"—they were able to do most everything in life, even though some in society could consider them old. By sixty, however, anyone still alive needed care to survive. If there was no family to provide that care, then it was the responsibility of the whole Christian community to make life possible and comfortable for those of such advanced age.

In such images as the care of the widows, one must emphasize a key New Testament theme toward the elderly. People of advanced age deserve the care of the community. It is a mandatory Christian responsibility to care for such elderly people. For early Christians, this did not fall into the sphere of civic duty. The government was not required to help people; the community of faith held the responsibility. The people of God who call themselves Christian in this first-century era consider themselves charged by God with providing the means of life for their whole people, including the youngest and the oldest. There is not necessarily a privilege attached to age; the right of care belongs to all those who hold membership in the community. One cannot "earn" care, and the New Testament does not emphasize the role of experience in teaching the next generation. In other words, the focus is not on the care that older people deserve; the New Testament focuses on the care that able-bodied Christians give to everyone in their community, regardless of age.

## The Value of Newness

In considering New Testament images of age, one must consider that early Christianity, to some extent, understood itself as a movement against the "old" ways of faith. To become a follower of Christ, these first Christians had to go against the teachings of their parents; they had to reject their elders' faith. In this sense, New Testament Christianity was a rebel movement that sometimes resembled a generational conflict. The New Testament expresses the tensions inherent in this embrace of newness through several metaphors about age and youth. Most striking are those in Paul's letters to the Corinthians.

> Clean out the old yeast so that you may be a new batch, as you really are unleavened. For our paschal lamb, Christ, has been sacrificed. Therefore, let us celebrate the festival, not with the old yeast, the yeast of malice and evil, but with the unleavened bread of sincerity and truth. (1 Cor. 5:7–8)

This passage is clearly metaphorical; Paul's concern is not yeast, but the actions of the Christians. Paul does not want the Corinthian Christians to fall into old ways, but instead to stay pure in their devotion to Christ and the new way of life that is theirs in Christ. Still, the use of age metaphors to make this point shows some of the underlying values of the early Christian community's rhetoric. Yeast is also a symbol of pre-Christian ways, both Jewish and pagan. But this yeast is specifically *old* yeast. It represents a previous way of doing things, a way learned through the generations and taught through parents and other elders. Instead of this old way, Paul insists on something new: the newness of Christianity, which was a way of life that was still "young" in the Christian's experience. Paul tells them to avoid the old ways in favor of the new, and this also means, to some extent, that one rejects the teachings of the elderly, traditional sources, in favor of new words against the old ways, spoken by younger people. Such was at least some Christian's experience at the movement's origins. An even stronger statement comes later in Paul's correspondence with this same church: "So if anyone is in Christ, there is a new creation: everything old has passed away; see, everything has become new!" (2 Cor. 5:17).

It is hard to read in such a verse any scriptural valuation of age and the elderly. Everything important is new; the old is valueless, replaced, discarded. Yet one must be careful not to read into Paul the values of our own times, when youth receives so much value, and the latest fad is always the biggest and the best. Certainly, this was not Paul's opinion, nor the point of his rhetoric. Instead, it is better to recognize that Paul connects newness (youth) and Christ's new creation in a different way. Paul doesn't say that everything young is good; he insists that everything in Christ is made new. Even the oldest members of the community, as influenced as they may be by old teachings that predate Christ, are made new through Christ's new creation.

Paul speaks of the power of change inherent in the Christian message. Paul recognizes that there are entrenched forces in the world that work against the Christian message, and some of these forces are supported by elderly people who insist on keeping things the way they have always been. There are times, Paul knows, when the status quo and those who defend it struggle against the gospel. But anyone, regardless of age, who becomes one with Christ accepts the newness that is the manifestation of the gospel. Age is never an impediment to the embrace of the gospel and the full participation in the body of Christ, because all are made new in God's new creation through Christ.

Still, Paul's message insists that everyone become new. This can be a special threat to the aging, who have learned much from long experience and have developed set ways of perceiving the world. The gospel does threaten everyone entrenched in other patterns of life. For the elderly, we must insist with Paul that Christ means change, a new creation that sweeps away old traditions, but we must also proclaim boldly the power of God to make all things new. A helpful example is the story of Elizabeth and Zechariah, the parents of the boy whom tradition remembers as John the

Baptist (Luke 1:5–25). Both of them are righteous and have been rewarded with long life, but they experience old age differently. In the temple performing priestly duties, Zechariah meets an angel who announces their upcoming parenthood. But Zechariah resists the changes that this would bring to his life; he argues and is made mute. Elizabeth, on the other hand, recognizes what is happening within her aging body, and she knows that it is God's work. She is willing to change and to embrace the changes that age brings—even when there are surprises.

Other parts of the New Testament are more clearly sympathetic to the role of the elderly. This probably represents the inevitable changes as Christianity moved from a first-generation religion (in which Christians had to reject the non-Christian ways of their youth and of their parents) to a second-generation religion. By the last third of the first century, there were many adult and aging Christians who had grown up as followers of Jesus, and so their whole lives were testaments to the faith. These elderly people had a wealth of experience gained from living decades as Christians in an often-hostile world, and over time that experience became one of the greatest assets to this still-growing movement of faith.

As Christians valued this experience, they increasingly honored the elders who carried the growing tradition in their minds, hearts, and bodies. The respect for elders is clear throughout the book of First Timothy, for example. The growing Christian community sought the experience of its elders, and they honored that experience as determinative for the church's life together. First Timothy 5:17 refers to elders who rule well, and who are thus worthy of double honor. To be old is not only to be experienced; age means authority, even the authority to rule other Christians.

Of course, these letters to Timothy represent later elements of New Testament thought, with a much more explicit concentration on the hierarchy involved. Not only are Christians learning to value the Christian experiences of the community's elders, but they are in the midst of controversy about how to organize themselves. First Timothy not only discusses the privileges assigned to elders in recognition for their experience but also sets the limits for hierarchical roles such as bishop and deacon. The church in this day was searching for rules about self-governance, in order to find the most reliable ways to make decisions about the community's present and future. The respect for elders means granting power within the community to the elders. By adopting such a pattern, the church embraced the social structure of the world, in which power flowed to those who were older and more experienced. The old problem still remained, however: those who had gained experience were often those who had invested themselves in the status quo. They were less likely to change, and more likely to accept cultural patterns without question. According to this late New Testament worldview, one accepts the ways of the world, at least to some extent, and that acceptance includes the valuation of elders. Unfortunately, it also meant a devaluation of the roles of women and others who were marginalized. Today's interpreter must walk a fine line, just as the early Christians did. We must respect the experience gained by elders without accepting the temptation to be entrenched in the world.

This fine line does reach expression in the early church, even if most of the expressions are indirect. For instance, consider 1 Tim. 5:19: "Never accept any accusation against an elder except on the evidence of two or three witnesses." On the one hand, there is an assumption that elders are pure. After all, they were not chosen hastily, and they came to their experience through a long and arduous process that deserves, and even demands, respect. On the other hand, even elders can sin. Experience and age are not immune to trouble. So the writer of the letter offers a balance. One assumes that elders are right, at least until there are more than one or two people who notice something amiss and are willing to confront the problem publicly. Elders are at the top of the hierarchical system, but they are not above the system, and they too must answer to the workings of the spirit among the assembled believers.

## Maturity

Perhaps a balance between the ultimate valuation of the new (as expressed in Christianity's newness) and an uncritical acceptance of the elders' rule (an accceptance the early church is shown approaching in documents such as 1 Timothy) comes in the New Testament's concept of maturity. Paul claims to speak wisdom only to the mature, even though such wisdom is not the wisdom of the day nor of the world's rulers (1 Cor. 2:6). In such a statement, Paul speaks against the power and wisdom that the world attaches to years and experience, while still valuing a maturity that must result from age, at least to some degree. Like the passage in Wisd. Sol. 4:7–9, discussed above, age is not by itself sufficient. Age imparts experience, and rightly used, this experience leads to wisdom and maturity, even though many people misunderstand their age-given experience and fail to attain such maturity. In other words, age alone does not make one mature. For Paul, the world and its powers never reach the maturity that Christians attain, and it is this maturity that allows the Christian—regardless of chronological age—to understand and live in the midst of God's own magnificent, mysterious wisdom.

Christians do not instantly achieve this maturity; it takes years of experience and faithful living. Sometimes the process is difficult. Thus, we can hear a New Testament writer crying out:

> We must no longer be children, tossed to and fro and blown about by every wind of doctrine, by people's trickery, by their craftiness in deceitful scheming. But speaking the truth in love, we must grow up in every way into him who is the head, into Christ. (Eph. 4:14–15)

Christians have a growth process that requires time and experience, and older Christians are more likely to have gone through this process that leads to maturity. Age may provide the time needed, but maturity requires more than years; it requires love and truth. Such is the mark of maturity, much more than gray hairs.[22]

Just as in Old Testament writing from ancient Israel, the New Testament speaks positively of age, even though it realizes that age is not an absolute good. When age becomes maturity, in the faith, it allows experience to keep the community vital and to provide it with necessary leadership and governance. But age also carries its troubles, especially for those whose years are spent living the power of the world instead of the foolishness of the gospel. There are times when such foolishness seems unspeakably young, and so, rightly, the mature in faith understand the wisdom of God, which is foolishness to the world even though it is the power of God to save all people, young and old alike. Age within the Christian community brings responsibility, and it brings honor and authority. At the same time, the New Testament encourages us never to forget the power of the gospel to make all things new, and to strive not for age and power in the ways of the world, but instead to work at whatever age toward a true maturity of the faith, embodying the truth and love at the heart of the gospel.

Five texts, examined in the sections that follow, offer specific insights into these tendencies within the Bible. One of the Ten Commandments deals specifically with the issue of care for the elderly. A strong valuing of flexibility and innovation is in one of Jesus' proverbs. A fascinating—and rather surprising—portrait of ripe old age occurs with David, the hero and king best known for his adventurous exploits of youth. There is the story of Elizabeth and Zechariah. And the book of Ecclesiastes closes with a meditation upon extreme age and approaching death that is striking in its frankness and realism. These five texts offer enhanced possibilities for understanding the biblical perspectives on aging and the elderly.

## Care for Parents:
## The Fifth Commandment

The fifth of the Ten Commandments offers an oft-repeated admonition: "Honor your father and your mother, so that your days may be long in the land that the LORD your God is giving you" (Ex. 20:12). Much modern interpretation, especially at the popular level, encourages us to think of this honoring as respect and obedience. When I was growing up, this was perhaps the most-enforced of the commandments. When I was five years old and in Sunday school, I wasn't really sure what a graven image and coveting even were, and both murder and adultery seemed out of the question (in fact, they were usually described as "commandments you'll need to know about when you get older"). But repeatedly I was told to respect and obey my parents. The context of the Old Testament's Ten Commandments was rather different from my own Sunday school experience. These instructions, like the legal codes throughout the Pentateuch, were established as binding upon adults. Adults should honor their parents. This changes the picture substantially. The clear goal is to encourage adults whose parents are still alive to provide for their elders' welfare. Many persons in early Israel, as well as the later years, would never have known their parents, but in cases where adult children had living parents, those parents would have been advanced in years. In the rural settings, that may have meant fifteen-year-old adults caring for thirty-year-old parents, but in that setting, thirty was an advanced age. The law requires children to provide care for their parents in such settings.

The parallels today are obvious, especially as we have a rapidly growing population of those whom culture considers as elderly persons. There is a responsibility incumbent upon each generation to provide care for its elders. In our own situation, this will prove to be of increasing expense, as the resources necessary to care for an older generation become more costly. But there is something more important than the expense to consider. The elderly have important experience to give, and society would be the poorer for ignoring those gifts.[23]

The Ten Commandments emphasize the result of following this law of caring for parents—it provides all people with opportunities for advanced age in the land. By caring for the elders, expertise and experience will be imparted to the whole people. The elderly have an important contribution to make, and the younger members of society must make sure that the elderly receive the care necessary for their contributions to continue throughout their lives. The success of the whole community—as well as its individual members—depends upon each member of the community contributing to that community and empowering others to make their best contributions. No society can long afford to disregard the offering of any segment of its population—and this is a lesson that our own world could profit from learning.

Of course, the Bible does not value age for age's sake. The elderly are expected to contribute to their society in the ways that they can. Younger people must provide the care necessary so that the elderly can make these contributions. The Old Testament has little patience for those who do not contribute to society, but it offers respect and protection for those with specific contributions, by encouraging others to enable the elderly to continue their special gifts to the whole people.

## The Problem
## with Old Wineskins

The Gospel of Matthew develops a proverb about the value of newness and the dangerous rigidity of the old.

> Then the disciples of John came to him, saying, "Why do we and the Pharisees fast often, but your disciples do not fast?" And Jesus said to them, "The wedding guests cannot mourn as long as the bridegroom is with them, can they? The days will come when the bridegroom is taken away from them, and then they will fast. No one sews a piece of unshrunk cloth on an old cloak, for the patch pulls away from the cloak, and a worse tear is made. Neither is new wine put into old wineskins; otherwise, the skins burst, and the wine is spilled, and the skins are destroyed; but new wine is put into fresh wineskins, and so both are preserved." (Matt. 9:14–17)

Matthew sets this story of Jesus as a response to a question by John's disciples, a question that (surprisingly) seems to state John the Baptist's preference for the Pharisees over Jesus. Jesus' reply makes a sharp point: he prefers to reject the tradition, and to do things in a different way than his predecessors, both John and the Pharisees. The "old" ways are out, and Jesus ushers in a new era, without fasting. The Gospel here speaks of Christianity as a rebel force that spurns the ways of the elders. Jesus and the disciples are new, "unshrunk," and "fresh." They cannot be combined with the old ways, for destruction would occur. New wine goes into new wineskins. New thoughts belong in new forms of expression. New movements embody themselves in young people who reject the old ways of their elders. This affirms the radical nature of Christianity in unflinching bluntness.

But this Gospel passage moves in other directions as well. Jesus' answer begins with a less familiar reply: "The days will come when the bridegroom is taken away from them, and then they will fast" (Matt. 9:15b). There is a place for the tradition of the elders; its time will come. One should not rush its time, just as one should not rush age, but its time comes, and then the prerogatives of age will be fitting. With this in mind, note again Jesus' concern: "Neither is new wine put into old wineskins; otherwise, the skins burst, and the wine is spilled, and the skins are destroyed" (Matt. 9:17).

The combination of new and old in inappropriate ways is wrong for three reasons: it destroys the old skins, it destroys the new wine, and it destroys the old skins. Put this way, the repetition, which is so easy to miss on first reading, becomes suddenly unmistakable. The text spends twice as much time concerned for the well-being of the old skins. These old skins are far from worthless; the text values them even more than the new wine. Combining old and new haphazardly destroys both.

What does this say about the place for old ideas in the church that was formed alongside these Gospel sayings? There is a place for both old and new (and for both young and old) in the church, and neither should take over the other. If either tries to subsume the other, then everything is destroyed and all is lost. Instead, each should keep its time and its place. Old customs (such as fasting) and youthful exuberance over the excitement of faith are both appropriate, and let them both occur. Let not the old customs swallow up the new; let not the new try to patch over the old. There are places for all.

Within this passage, there is yet another positive image of elders. Of course, there is a value in the old wineskins. Luke (at least in most manuscripts) adds the key point at the conclusion of the wineskins passage: "And no one after drinking old wine desires new wine, but says, 'The old is good'" (Luke 5:39). Despite the joys of newness and the need for radical change in the beginnings of faith, there is still an abiding worth in the oldest parts of the community, and in the end the oldest is best.

## The Elder David

David is best known for his youthful exploits. In Sunday school, in children's sermons, and from the pulpit we tell of the young, naive, undefended David defeating the larger (and more experienced and older) Goliath. David was a swashbuckler and a womanizer, a man at home in ancient Israel's golden palaces and on today's silver screens. But David ruled as king for more than four decades, and he lived to an old age that he put to use. He was just as much king when he was sixty as when he was still in his twenties—even though the stories of his old age are less popular today than those of his youth.

David's youthful vigor and refreshing naïveté gave way to an aged wisdom by the end of his reign. Second Samuel 23:2–7 records his last words:

> The spirit of the LORD speaks through me, God's word is upon my tongue. The God of Israel has spoken, the Rock of Israel has said to me: One who rules over people justly, ruling in the fear of God, is like the light of morning, like the sun rising on a cloudless morning, gleaming from the rain on the grassy land. Is

not my house like this with God? For God has made with me an everlasting covenant, ordered in all things and secure. Will God not cause to prosper all my help and my desire? But the godless are all like thorns that are thrown away; for they cannot be picked up with the hand; to touch them one uses an iron bar or the shaft of a spear. And they are entirely consumed in fire on the spot. (NRSV, modified)

In age, David knows God's word, and he encourages Israel's future kings to rule in justice and in close relationship with God, avoiding the godlessness that would plague the monarchy throughout much of its history. David the king, foolish in youthful energy, grows into the wisdom of age and understands the true nature of God's intentions for the monarchy, even if it takes him until his last words to do so.

But in order to attain such wisdom, one needs more than time. One needs the care of others. People live to old age and acquire such wisdom only when others work to care for them and to provide for their physical, emotional, and spiritual needs. David needed others to care for his needs throughout his waning years. David reached an advanced age, and his abilities were significantly limited. The contributions of wisdom do not come without a price, and the Old Testament does not shirk from the admission that there are things that the elderly, wise though they may be, cannot do and do not know. A new king, Adonijah, had crowned himself in David's place, and David wasn't even aware of it. David's closest advisors, Nathan and Bathsheba, explained the situation to him and encouraged his correct action to assure that Solomon would be the next king. Through a coalition of persons such as Nathan and Bathsheba, as well as the aging David, good government prevailed.

But David had needs other than good advice, and the Old Testament refers to those needs in ways that can make one blush. So begins the book of First Kings:

> King David was old and advanced in years; and although they covered him with clothes, he could not get warm. So his servants said to him, "Let a young virgin be sought for my lord the king, and let her wait on the king, and be his attendant; let her lie in your bosom, so that my lord the king may be warm." So they searched for a beautiful girl throughout all the territory of Israel, and found Abishag the Shunammite, and brought her to the king. The girl was very beautiful. She became the king's attendant and served him, but the king did not know her sexually.

Although this hardly would make for effective nursing-home policy today, it reflects a concern for the elderly that is striking. Their every need should be met. David still had service to perform, even if he did not know everything that was going on around him. It would not do to have the king freeze to death because of his age and failing circulation; people needed to care for him in ways that were effective. They needed to keep his heart pumping, and they found that young, beautiful Abishag kept David warm and comfortable. Texts such as this show a much wider definition of the needs of the elderly than many segments of today's society—including the church—are willing to admit. The needs for companionship, advice, and meaningful contribution, as well as needs for physical care, are all present. Neglecting any of these needs would be as criminal and as destructive to the society as ignoring any of the others. The society needs the contributions of its elders and must meet their social and physical needs so that these benefits can be shared with the whole people.

## Elizabeth and Zechariah:
## A Model of Age's Benefits and Dangers

Perhaps Elizabeth and Zechariah best symbolize the ambivalence about age in the New Testament. Luke's Gospel introduces the reader to these fascinating characters at the start of Jesus' story. These two were blameless people who lived in God's own presence. We hear not once but twice (Luke 1:7, 18) that this couple was old—very old. Their age, in fact, becomes the turning point of the story, as an angel appears and announces Elizabeth's upcoming pregnancy.

Their age is essential, especially in comparison to Mary, Elizabeth's young cousin who also finds herself surprisingly pregnant. Elizabeth and Zechariah are accustomed to the temple, as a result of their experience and age. To be sure, Zechariah shows plenty of shock at the news that he would soon be a father, but Elizabeth is able to name what has happened to her: "This is what the Lord has done for me" (Luke 1:25). Her age and experience combine so that she knows the Lord's presence. Elizabeth experiences the Holy Spirit in her own body and shouts aloud the good news (Luke 1:41–42). Because she is old enough to know and to understand, she can explain to young Mary, who hears Elizabeth's teaching and issues forth her own song of praise (Luke 1:46–55). The elderly Elizabeth uses her advantage of age to mentor Mary. Age speaks of God, whom the elders have known for decades, and age teaches youth to sing God's praise.

But in Zechariah, age is silence. Zechariah does not believe the angel (Luke 1:20) and is silenced. His age teaches him disbelief and rejects what is new and unexpected. Even when he sees the angel face to face and feels God's own presence, his mind is locked in the past and he accepts nothing new. He speaks again only when he names the child as God's gift (Luke 1:63), for such is the meaning of young John's name. As soon as Zechariah writes the name, he too joins in the speech that praises God—the same speech first sung by Elizabeth and next by Mary. Elizabeth's age prepares her to see God, and Zechariah's age blinds him.[24] Still, in the end, they both praise, joining their voices with young Mary.

Age is good when it brings wisdom, and bad when it brings intransigent resistance to God's radical newness. Youth is full of fear, for there is much that youth has not seen, but youth at its best is receptive to the witness about God found on the lips of the best of age. Perhaps in this image of singing and silence one hears a faint echo of a more ancient Zechariah, a prophet who sang forth God's vision:

> Thus says the LORD of hosts: Old men and old women shall again sit in the streets of Jerusalem, each with staff in hand because of their great age. And the streets of the city shall be full of boys and girls playing in its streets. Thus says the LORD of hosts: Even though it seems impossible to the remnant of this people in these days, should it also seem impossible to me, says the LORD of hosts? (Zech. 8:4–6)

## Approaching Death:
## Ecclesiastes

The story of David honestly depicts the needs and limitations of the elderly; Zechariah and Elizabeth teach of age's value. The book of Ecclesiastes, a skeptical work throughout, closes with an extended meditation on the discomforts and discomfitures of aging. Truly, the elderly are full of wisdom and values to share with the entire community, but Ecclesiastes knows that the days of elderly life have an end, and for all people, no matter what their value, that end is death.

> Remember your creator in the days of your youth, before the days of trouble come, and the years draw near when you will say, "I have no pleasure in them"; before the sun and the light and the moon and the stars are darkened and the clouds return with the rain; in the day when the guards of the house tremble, and the strong men are bent, and the women who grind cease working because they are few, and those who look through the windows see dimly; when the doors on the street are shut, and the sound of the grinding is low, and one rises up at the sound of a bird, and all the daughters of song are brought low; when one is afraid of heights, and terrors are in the road; the almond tree blossoms, the grasshopper drags itself along and desire fails; because all must go to their eternal home, and the mourners will go about the streets;

before the silver cord is snapped, and the golden bowl is broken, and the pitcher is broken at the fountain, and the wheel broken at the cistern, and the dust returns to the earth as it was, and the breath returns to God who gave it. (Eccl. 12:1–7)

This passage's metaphors talk of the end of life as days of trouble, honestly recognizing the onset of physical limitations. One's vision dims, and one's hearing can be lost. It becomes difficult to stand as straight and tall as once was possible. The loss of physical prowess can bring one to fear. Menopause and impotence may plague the elderly, changing their self-concepts. The silver cord snaps; the gold bowl breaks; the pitcher cracks. Dust returns to dust, and breath returns to God.

In the midst of this refreshing and sobering honesty comes a valuation of life that stands firm in the face of death. Even though death batters the body and weakens what once was, life is still valuable. The cord is still silver; the bowl is still golden, even if brittle and breakable. The oldest life is still life, and it is still very valuable. At the end, breath returns to God. We have lived life empowered by that breath, and God's breath is not wasted. It returns to God, who welcomes back the value of our lives, not disdaining the life that was once stronger or more vibrant.

And, of course, while God's breath remains in us, we are still fully human, and we are still fully inspired and empowered by that divine breath. Through the last minute of life, God's presence is still full, and even death is but return. Age is a time of contribution, just as is youth, even though youth's contributions are physical and the offerings of the aging and elderly must often take other forms. God's presence remains the same, and the gift of life with God does not diminish even in the face of the body's inexorable march to return to dust. Perhaps we are nothing but a puff of breath—but that breath is God's, and it will return. For now, there is effort and contribution, and life.[25]

**SERMON**

# Remembering and Reconciling

Jon L. Berquist

*Occasion for sermon:* "Remembering and Reconciling" is a sermon for remembering longtime members. An earlier version of this sermon was preached to a congregation of the Christian Church (Disciples of Christ) in Oklahoma on June 12, 1994. The texts from 2 Cor. 5:16–21 and 1 Samuel 16 were part of the lectionary for that Sunday. This congregation was celebrating those in its midst who had been members for fifty years or longer, so it was an appropriate time to reflect on the values of older persons in the life of the church. The congregation had also requested its pastor's resignation a few weeks earlier. The sermon was intended to work within these situations: a lectionary text praising the new, the church's celebration of its elderly members, and the congregation's wariness about its own future.

We gather today for a celebration—a remembrance of the pillars of this church. For the last fifty years, this congregation has counted on this collection of members. Fifty years ago others were here as well, and now there are still others in these pews who have joined much more recently. Despite all the change over a half century, good and bad alike, these members have been faithful. For this, we give God thanks, and we rightly honor these valuable members of Christ's body.

It's important to *remember*, especially in the midst of this changing world, where all too often we forget. The world tempts us to forget, to overlook the values of the past, and to think that only the newest and latest is what matters. We hear it from the television, from politicians, from seemingly everyone: new is best. But we need to remember.

Remembering keeps us together. Remembering builds the bonds and bridges that connect us. But the lectionary today gives us a strange text for this celebration of remembering. Paul seems to revel in newness. "If anyone is in Christ, there is a new creation: everything old has passed away; see, everything has become new!" Doesn't Paul value the traditions, the standards, the stalwarts of faith? Does Paul fall prey to the cultural rush to the new? Does Paul forget to remember?

Listen to Paul again. "Everything has become new." *Everything*—even the old. Paul never rejects the old, because he knows that God transforms everything, from the oldest to the newest. God uses and transforms the child, even the newest infant in the nursery or sitting in a parent's lap, and God uses and transforms the fifty-year members, keeping them ever-new through their continuing service. Paul knows that we recognize people today not only because they were here fifty years ago, but because they are here *now*. Now, in the midst of new times, old-time members and new ones join together to form God's church, and God uses us all in powerful ways, taking each change in this congregation's life and making it new. And all the newness starts where it always starts—with the oldest members of the church, the stalwarts, the pillars, the solid foundation upon which so much has been built.

We need to remember. We need to remember the old stories of the faith, like those told in the Bible, and the not-so-old stories of the faith, such as those about the people here, who have served so well over five decades. Remembering calls us all together, in the service of the living

God, to be the church right here and right now. And right now, it is right to remember the past, and to celebrate it.

In fact, it is right to remember a lot of stories. We could spend hours remembering the stories of our honored members in the congregation, but let me share an even older story this morning. It's a story of David. We tell so many of David's stories, and we especially love to tell the stories of David's feisty youth, when everything went well for him and he won victories everywhere he turned. Visions of Goliath fill our heads, as the giant towers over our young hero; we urge the underdog on to victory, rejoicing with him when he wins on behalf of all his people. We like the stories of David's victories, and we love to tell those old, old stories in sermons and Sunday schools. But there are other stories of David, and we don't like those stories as much. David had a dark side; sometimes he moved in directions we do not respect. These stories are part of David, too, and they are also part of our own story, for even the greatest examples of the faith had their failings.

The Bible nudges us toward one of the less pleasant stories, but this is part of remembering just the same. In 1 Samuel 15 and 16, we begin with two other characters, Saul and Samuel. Saul was the king before David, a mighty warrior; Samuel was the prophet and judge who anointed Saul to be king. But Saul, as it turned out, was a sinner. He was failed and fallen—just like us. And after one particularly sad and sinful incident, God decided it was time for a change, for a new king who would arise in the land. Samuel had genuinely liked Saul, even though their relationship had hit rough times. Saul wasn't perfect, but he had certainly done a lot for his people, hadn't he? Wasn't that worth something? And yet it was time to move on. We all face change. Sometimes the change feels right and good; we call it progress, and it opens new vistas before our eyes. Sometimes change is frightening and terrifying. It seems to threaten everything we've built. Our whole lives fall prey to the suddenness of changing events—a car accident, or corporate downsizing, or a heart attack, or a mistake that never gets forgiven. Something happens all of a sudden, and then everything changes, for good or for bad, or both. In this story of Samuel and Saul, as in all the stories of our lives, the past begins to fade away, and sometimes we're sad to see it go so soon.

David enters the story only at the end, as the least likely one to be chosen as the next king. But the story hinges not on David, or even on Saul. We hear that God was sorry that Saul had ever been king; looking back on it, even God thought it had all been a mistake. So God turns to Samuel and says: "How long will you grieve over Saul?"

Because we love those stories of David so well, we're eager to keep going through the story. If you peek ahead, Goliath is waiting just a page or so away; chapter 17 tells his story with all its seductive fervor. But we're in chapter 16, and it starts out, "How long will you grieve?" Life has changed; the old has passed away; behold, the new has come. There's no way forward, except through the grief. "How long will you grieve?" How should we answer that question? Samuel stands before God, caught between the great and falling Saul and the young boy David, not yet ready to be king. The question haunts us when we face those unavoidable, miserable changes. "How long?"

Don't push the grief away. Let it last. Saul has done wonderful things, and the memory of the past lingers. Don't push it away—it's good to remember, even when not all the memories are happy ones. Remember what went wrong; remember the dreams dashed on the rocky shores of reality; grieve the loss of what might have been but now will never be again. Accept the grief; admit it; share it with the others who mourn the passage of hopes, the loss of opportunity, the funeral of the past. Feel the grief and give it words. But don't let the grief last forever. Grief is necessary, for it is the way to remember, but the story goes on. Let the grief last, for a chapter. Keep on with the story, a story that goes forth out of grief into a new future, a new creation.

But wait a minute—the grief lasts more than a chapter. When Samuel finds David and announces him as the next king, the proclamation is over in an instant, but there's still a long way to go. For the rest of First Samuel, David is a king-in-training. The new future doesn't start all of a sudden. David battles his way to the kingship, and there is a great cost. He grieves his way into a new future, and even in 2 Samuel 1, when David achieves the victory and becomes king, he sings his lament for Saul. Grief does not pass away quickly, but the new world is coming. We must admit our grief at every loss. Grief lasts. Grief endures to shape our memories of what we have lost. Grief will pass, but not until we have grappled with it and given grief its due. Hold fast to the hope that a new world is coming, but don't deny or delay the work of grief to prepare the way to that new future.

What does David do when the grief ends? He builds a new kingdom. Saul was king, then David became king. Saul had an army; David had a bigger, better army. Saul ruled over a large and mighty nation; David expanded the borders and made the nation even bigger. In every way that Saul was king, David was king—and more. And we who watch David's rise to power should not be too surprised to find that his brave new kingdom had the same old problems. As a youth, David was the bright shining future, but as king he made the same mistakes. The kingdom could start over from scratch. Everything could be made right again. But David's role wasn't any better. Again, the dreams and hopes were broken. Starting over wasn't enough.

And that's why God offers us a new creation. It's more than just starting over. God gives us a way to experience something truly new and truly different, something beyond the experiences of the past. God offers a new creation that wipes away the old kingdoms and solves the old problems. But it's hard. It's hard because we like the old ways. We made those old problems with our sweat and blood; we invested ourselves in the old ways of doing things that brought us to this point. We like the old ways, and we're stubborn in our sinfulness. But God offers a new creation, with the old problems removed. It's something truly new, and it means that we have to stop the problems that we've made. The old ways may have been comfortable, but we must do things differently if we wish to keep the mistakes of history from repeating themselves. David chose to keep on doing what had been done before—a new person in charge, new faces all around, but the same old thing. God offers a new creation—new people, new ideas, a new future, a new way of being together.

It's a risk, but it's a chance for new life. As Paul says, "everything old has passed away." Well, not everything—our founders are still here, and our memories still remind us to celebrate the wonderful things of the past. But in God's new creation there is a commitment to move ahead. We never *replace* the past; we *embrace* the past as we move together toward something new, something different. We have grieved long enough, and now we bury our grief and our resentment and walk away from it. The pains of the past can no longer hurt us. In God's new creation, we leave behind our stubbornness and our pride and our habits of making the same mistakes over again. We even let our nostalgia pass away, for we feel God's presence not only in the glories of a proud past, but even more so in the future ahead. That's the miracle of the new creation—it's not that the past was so bad, but that God's future is so spectacular that it calls us forward, and we leave behind the griefs and the pains and the habits of problems that have set us back over and over again. The new creation calls us forward to new things that God has in store for us.

And in that new creation, everything is new—from the youngest members to the oldest generation of most honored members. Everything is new, for it's the chance for everyone to start over. The oldest members are not lost; they are not set aside and forgotten. They are remembered and brought to the center and made new. And it's new because it's reconciled to God. What we remembered is now reconciled. That means that God has set our priorities straight as a church and as each individual. We are experiencing God's new reconciliation. We're lined up on a path to God's future. We remember the glories of the past, and we take that past with us as we point ourselves toward the future. That's the miracle of God's new creation.

Not only do we live in the miracle of the new creation, but we preach it to the rest of the world. The church demonstrates its newness to everyone around. We show that we are a new creation, reconciled to God, connected to the past and pointed toward the future. As Paul says, God has reconciled us and given us the ministry of reconciliation. That means growing beyond our pain, but always remembering our past and knowing the pain of the world. God does not call us to forget the past in order to be part of the new; God calls us all, old and new alike, to enter into a fresh path. God calls us to move through our pain and beyond it. For God knows that grief takes time, and that even David must grieve, and so must we. Only in the midst of the change, the grief, the pain—only there do we find the opportunity for reconciliation that calls us forward.

As we take hold of the reconciliation, as God makes us new right before our eyes, we become ambassadors of a God who will make everything new. God is making an appeal through us. Through *us!* Through the people who grieve, God reaches out to a world that grieves, to proclaim newness, to demonstrate the power of reconciliation, to announce that we are new people because we live in the life-changing reality of God's grace. We live as new people, who have passed through the fires of grief only to stand firm as God's own representatives to this world.

God has not forgotten us. We celebrate our past today, and we are right to remember, for God remembers us with the same mixture of pride and grief that we feel. God remembers us, the good and the bad alike, and God reconciles us, pointing us ahead. God remembers to make us new.

We remember all the stories. We remember David, and Saul, and Samuel, of countless generations ago. We remember the leaders of this church for the past fifty years. We remember the new tragedies, and we remember the new hope for a new creation brought about by our reconciliation that God remembers to enact in our midst.

So we go forward. We move ahead to build a new kingdom where God can work through us, knowing that we will make the same mistakes as before, even though we strive to start over. But more than that—much, much more than that—we go forward in the experience of God's new creation, where everything is made new. God reconciles us—to ourselves, to each other, to our past, and also to the whole world. As the new creation, we preach Christ, and we live Christ's reconciling power in our own lives.

# 5

# Waiting on the Lord:
# Reflecting on Scripture
# near the End of Life

*Cynthia M. Campbell*

Preaching is always an interaction between text and preacher within a particular context. Just as "new occasions teach new duties" (as James Russell Lowell wrote), so preaching in distinctly different circumstances can teach the preacher new things about the Word of God and about the preacher's own faith. Preaching to persons who are near the end of their lives represents a significant challenge for the preacher, both as person and as theologian. In this chapter I will reflect on "content" more than "method" in preaching because the preacher must know first of all what she or he wants to say before a judgment can be made about how to say it.

The basis for this particular reflection is the pastoral context of a midsized Presbyterian congregation in central Kansas. The median age of the membership was over fifty. Nearly one hundred members lived in care facilities or were effectively homebound. On average the pastoral staff conducted thirty-five to forty funerals per year. Regular duties also included preaching once a month at Sunday worship for the residents in the healthcare portion of the retirement home in the town.

Some might find this a depressing situation. But preaching in an aging congregation, in nursing homes as well as at funerals, can enable the preacher to reflect on her or his own future and on mortality. It can lead the preacher into deeper reflection on both the goodness of life and the reality of grace. It can convince the preacher, and (we hope) the congregation, of the importance of each day of life and confirm the confidence that both present and future belong not to us but to God.

As background for this chapter, I asked some retirement home residents to reflect on their experience of worship in that setting as well as in funeral services. Representing as they did long years of faithful worship attendance, these people shared fascinating insights in worship, preaching, and faith from the vantage point of those who see themselves as nearing the end of life. Four were Presbyterians; the other three were Methodists.

In conversations such as these, the preacher can meet Simeon and Anna: people of faith who face their daily lives as glad and hopeful believers. They are realistic about death and yet confident. In their lifetimes, they have known the emptiness of the Great Depression, the horrors of two world wars, and the sweeping cultural changes that are hard for all of us to comprehend. And yet, their attitude about life is one of hope. As one man said, "I want to live until I die." Many in this group were people who read two newspapers every day and subscribe to at least a dozen magazines.

To be sure, not all older people meet life in this manner. For some the challenges of poor health or reduced material circumstances, or difficult family situations bring depression, guilt, remorse, and unresolved grief. Those circumstances, too, must be addressed. But the themes to be considered here are precisley those which can aid even these troubled others to find the hope that makes life possible.

## Themes for Preaching

### Old and New

One thing older people find helpful is a balance between the familiar and the new. This is true in worship as a whole as well as in preaching. Familiar texts and "the old songs" provide comfort and continuity with the past. But most older people do not want to live in the past. As a matter of fact, they are quite aware that they do *not* live there and then. Where they live is here and now.

What is wanted and needed is a way for the past to be a resource for interpreting and understanding the present. People who are now in their seventies, eighties, and nineties have lived through changes that are almost literally incredible. They were born in a world where the automobile was revolutionary; in a world dominated by European colonial governments; in a world of large and extended families, often tied to a particular region or even neighborhood.

They live now in a world of space travel and car phones; in a world where it is hard to keep up with changes on the international map; and in a world where they themselves are often separated by great distances from most if not all family members. To be sure, these changes are sometimes met with fear, hostility, and denial. Change can cause bewilderment and anxiety. There are those who firmly believe that some time in the past, things really were not only easier but better.

But lots of older people also know that you can't go back, and you can't go home again. They know that the world has changed and will change more. What they want and need (as do all people) is a way to think about and respond to these changes from within the perspective of faith.

The biblical faith has two very interesting answers to this problem. On the one hand, it affirms that God is "the same yesterday, today, and forever." The psalmist proclaims that, though everything else should change, God remains our refuge and strength (Ps. 46:1), the "mighty fortress." On the other hand, the Bible also shows us the God who says, "I am about to create new heavens and a new earth; the former things shall not be remembered or come to mind" (Isa. 65:17).

The God who was there at the beginning is the same as the God who will be there at the end, and yet the beginning and the end are not the same. Constancy of purpose and transformation are both part of God's plan. One of the goals of preaching, then, is to help people for whom change seems drastic to make sense of that change as part of God's continual creating and sustaining work.

### Christian Hope

A second theme is closely related. Those near the end of life have all of life, both personal and cultural, on which to reflect. Some people become mired in the past, full of regret or stuck in denial that now is not then. But many say that while they want to remember the good from the past, their real concern is hope for the future.

For some, hope for the future has to do with their personal future. They are faced by many questions: How will I face disease and suffering? How will I live if I outlive my spouse or close sibling or special friend or children? What is there beyond this life? All these questions address real and important issues. But many older people are clear that they want hope that goes far beyond the personal.

What is the Christian hope on a cosmic scale? What do Christians have to say about the future of humanity? about the survival of the planet? about the world their great-grandchildren will inherit? Eschatology is not an easy concept for many Christians. Some preachers are troubled by the Advent lectionary and its emphasis on "the end of time" or the "second coming of Christ." Others will admit great reluctance to preach from the Revelation to John.

Part of the discomfort is the legitimate theological conviction that Christian discipleship involves living and working in this world today so as to shape the future in accordance with God's purposes. Faithfulness and obedience imply concrete actions in the world through which we work alongside God in bringing God's realm "on earth as it is in heaven." But responding to the questions of those near the end of life reminds us that the future doesn't really belong to us. It belongs to God.

The basis of Christian hope does not lie in our ability to shape the future. Christian hope rests on that affirmation that God is in the future as well as in the present. The Reformed tradition in particular has stressed that both human history and the natural order are governed by the plan and purpose of God (the doctrine of providence). People who know they are close to the end of their personal histories often say that they long to be reminded that there is a history that will go on without them to some larger destiny, and that this destiny is in the hands of a loving and redeeming God.

### Encouragement

A third theme for preaching is "encouragement." It is an old saying that the preacher's task is to comfort the afflicted and afflict the comfortable. But encouragement is even deeper than comfort. "Be of good cheer! Hold fast to what is good! Fear not! Rejoice in the Lord!" Paul's letters are full of words of encouragement to the communities of new Christians. He speaks as one a little farther ahead on the mountain trail, calling back over his shoulder: Keep on coming! We're getting there! Don't give up! You can do it! In order to be fruitfully and faithfully alive, human beings have a deep need to feel that their lives have a purpose. After a life-threatening illness, it is not uncommon to hear people say, "God must still have something for me to do, otherwise I wouldn't still be here." Embedded in that sentiment is the theological affirmation that God calls all people to discipleship and service. It states the conviction that God has a purpose for each and every human life.

Obviously, near the end of life one deals with diminished capacity of various types. One is no longer as strong or quick or able as in the past. Sometimes interests change with abilities. Part of the task of living at this stage is making peace with these changes, but an equally important task is affirming what one can do and who one can be at this particular time.

Simply put, older people need to be reminded of the goodness of life and of the goodness and value of their own lives. A sense of personal self-worth is necessary for anyone, and the lack of it can lead to depression or even self-destructive behavior. There are at least two ways to affirm self-worth: first, by helping folk recall the value and contribution they have made in the past, and second, by helping them see that there are contributions they can still make to the world in which they live. For instance, it is important to remind those who are no longer active volunteers in the life of the church that they can make a great contribution by praying regularly for the work of the church, for its members, and for its staff. They can write notes or check in with others by phone. Especially for those who live in a communal setting, such as a retirement home or nursing facility, there are hundreds of opportunities to show compassion, care, love, and support— both for neighbors and for staff. Discipleship remains a real possibility, and fulfilling that call is both the right thing to do and a factor that contributes to a sense of self-worth.

One older person observed that especially helpful to her are stories of how others have met the challenges of growing older. Encouragement often comes from knowing the experiences of those who have traveled the path ahead of us. For some of us, this might mean becoming more familiar with the great saints of the church. For others, it is a matter of listening carefully to one another's stories.

### Incarnation

Several theological or biblical themes recur frequently throughout the church year. While they are not unique in importance to older persons, it takes only a little imagination to see how they relate to this population.

The first is incarnation. The heart of the Christian confession is that God was incarnate in Jesus of Nazareth, called the Christ. In this human life, the fullness of God was pleased to dwell. All that is human is taken up into the life of God. Through the incarnation God can be seen to identify or be in solidarity with all that is human and with every human person.

Among the many implications of this basic faith affirmation is the question of where we are to look for God and God's presence in our lives. Because God chose to live with us as one of us, we are called to continue looking for God in those who are around us. Because we are baptized into Christ and become members of Christ's body, our calling is to continue Christ's work through our own lives. It is easy to feel that we find God when we look to the beauty of nature. The Christian gospel calls us as well to look into the eyes and hearts and lives of those around us and there find the image of the invisible God, the presence of the living Christ.

This theme can have special meaning to those whose lives seem confined, for while the number of their contacts with others may be diminished, the importance of them is not. Also at the end of life, it may be important to take time to savor special family relations or to repair damage done earlier in life. Both of those tasks can be emphasized as we remind those listening to us that it is precisely in those others around us that we have the opportunity to see God or to meet Christ and to *be* Christ for others.

### Living This Day

One of the standard responses for the opening of worship is, "This is the day which the Lord has made; let us rejoice and be glad in it." Much has been written about the importance of living in the moment. People concerned about stress reduction, therapists dealing with relationship problems, and those who teach various meditation techniques all emphasize the benefits of attending to the here and now. We do better as humans when we let go of the past (especially when it is filled with pain or remorse) and when we lay aside anxiety about the future.

Living in the present and valuing the present moment is good psychological advice. It is also the proper response of faith. This is the day *God* has given us. The time and circumstance of this day are in our hands to be used (and enjoyed) in faithful stewardship to God. For the older person especially there can be both great comfort and real liberation in being reminded to live in the here and now. In fact, dwelling on the past (whether that was a good or a painful time) or peering anxiously into an unknown future rob one of the ability to live and thrive in the moment one does have.

This is not to say that memory is not of vital importance. But life is for this day and not for a day that is past. *This* is the day God gives each of us. This is the only day we really "have" in which to glorify and serve God and to begin enjoying God forever. This relates to the themes above, for *this* is the day when we can respond to God's call and know God's affirming and redeeming presence.

### Grace

Finally, we turn to the theme of grace. As the best-known hymn in the English language puts it: "Grace has brought me safe thus far, and grace will lead me home." Another less familiar hymn (words attributed to John Calvin) says: "Thou art the life by which alone we live, and all our substance and our strength receive." The heirs to that tradition believe that grace is not only the source of creation—grace is that which sustains all life, all things, in each and every moment of existence. God is not only the Creator but also the gracious preserver of all that is.

Such a notion of the life-giving and life-sustaining power of God is a theme of great strength and comfort, especially for those whose personal strength may be waning. As we face difficulties or pain or danger, as we deal with losses and grief, as we struggle with loneliness, the word of God is that grace (God's unmerited love and favor) will sustain us now as it has sustained us in the past.

The most recent confession of faith written by the Presbyterian Church (U.S.A.) begins: "In life and in death, we belong to God." It concludes: " . . . nothing in life or in death can separate us from the love of God in Christ Jesus our Lord." To say that our lives are in God's hand (that we belong not to ourselves but to God) is to affirm the prevenient grace of God. Reformed theologians shaped this doctrine from the biblical affirmation that God will never break the covenants God has made with humankind. Whether we live or whether we die, God will always be faithful to us. In life *and* in death, we will always belong to God.

All these themes are from the heart of Christian tradition. They are life-shaping concepts for all people, not just for those who are older. But anyone who has lived and worked with older persons will be struck by how much these themes relate to the experience of older persons and how much they have to teach us about these matters if we will but listen. Of course, not all older people are blessed with deep and abiding faith. But many are, and the witness they have to give can be of great strength and encouragement to the rest of us.

## Preaching in Nursing- or
## Retirement-Home Settings

In preparing sermons for older adults and particularly those who live in nursing homes or retirement situations, keep in mind a few practical comments about such worship. Especially in nursing-home settings, the ability of people to remain attentive or to follow a worship service may be limited. As one person put it, what is most important for some is simply to have had the "feeling" of being in church, whether they follow all of the service or not.

In leading worship in such settings, remember that worship should be long enough to be meaningful but short enough to accommodate limited attention span and ability to sit comfortably in one position. Obviously, it is important for the preacher to be heard. Preachers do well to remember that the most effective aid to hearing is not amplification; it is diction. Finally, worship in such settings requires some elements of familiarity, such as choosing familiar scripture passages and hymns. Learning which songs are known by memory by at least some in the worshiping group can be of great aid to the worship leader in planning a service.

## The Challenge of
## the Funeral Sermon

Thus far, the focus has been on the ordinary task of preaching in a Sunday or midweek service. We now turn to the particular issue of preaching at a memorial service or funeral. Most funerals are conducted for older persons, and many who come to such services are also older persons.

Many funerals or memorial services begin with the words: "Our help is in the name of the Lord who made heaven and earth. We are here to worship God and give thanks to God for the life of . . ." The emphasis of such a service, like any worship experience, should be the worship of God. God is the primary object of our attention because it is God who is to be thanked for the life of the one who has died. Keeping God as the center of worshiping attention accomplishes two things. First, it puts our living and dying in the kind of perspective discussed above ("in life and in death, we belong to

God"). Second, it shifts the focus from the tragedy of loss or from sentimental recall to the goodness of God in giving life and the promise of God to care for life. Centering the funeral service on God frees the congregation to remember with gratitude the good that has passed from one life to others, with confidence in God's continuing presence both to survivors and to the one who has died.

As we experience it, a funeral service is, from a human point of view, conducted for the benefit of the living. Preaching in such a context can all too easily slip into sentimental tribute or the opportunity to make doctrinal points about judgment, repentance, the afterlife, and so on. Neither of those is helpful or theologically responsible. If the purpose of the service is to worship God in the context of the celebration of a particular human life, the sermon must be focused accordingly. One thing that a sermon in this setting can do is to gather up what can be learned from one person's journey in life and let that story bring meaning, hope, and encouragement to the lives of others.

The text for preaching, however, is always the Bible, not one person's life. It is the Word of God that nourishes faith, and the experiences we bring are illustrative at best. The preacher preparing a sermon of this type is well advised to visit at length with family and friends after someone has died and to gather from them memories and impressions of their friend. By reflecting on these conversations, the preacher may then turn to scripture and look for a word or theme that needs to be said for this life and for the situation of this particular death. At times, it is obvious that a person's life story draws us to certain theological ideas. At other times, the circumstances surrounding the death or the family relationships call for a particular word. The attempt is to let the biblical tradition speak to the unique situation of living and dying that is now celebrated before God.

## "Waiting on the Lord"

The end of life is not (and should not be) "waiting around" for the call that never comes. Most older people want to be active, if they are able, and engaged in the business of living as long as they are alive. "Waiting on the Lord" refers to rhetoric from the psalmists, who remind all of us of the way we should live: "For God alone my soul waits in silence; from God comes my salvation. God alone is my rock and my salvation, my fortress; I shall never be shaken" (Ps. 62:1–2). "I wait for the LORD, my soul waits, and in God's word I hope; my soul waits for the Lord more than those who watch for the morning" (Ps. 130:5–6).

Waiting for the Lord is the attitude of the hopeful and prayerful soul before God. It is an attitude of trust but also of expectation. As an old psalter paraphrase puts it, "my soul with expectation doth depend on God

indeed." Expectation is an active attitude. It speaks of eyes open, mind
alert, antennae out. To "wait" in this sense is to live paying attention to
what is going on and, in particular, to what God is doing. Expectation is
hopeful anticipation, and its opposite is dread. It is not accidental that "expecting" is the old euphemism for pregnancy, because it is precisely the anticipation of new life.

Anna and Simeon were waiting for the Lord. Their days were spent in
the temple, "looking forward to the consolation of Israel" (Luke 2:25). Perhaps that is one of the roles we can appreciate and cultivate among believers
who are closer to the end of their lives than some of the rest of us. Perhaps
at that stage it can become clearer for what and for whom one waits. Perhaps those persons will be among the most able to lead us all in this basic
attitude of living and praying: to wait with joyful anticipation for the presence of God.

SERMON

# A Witness to Hope

Cynthia M. Campbell

*Occasion for sermon:* This "teaching sermon" was preached on Memorial Day, the Seventh Sunday after Easter in 1990. The texts selected were
among those often read at funeral or memorial services (Psalm 130; Isa.
43:1–7; 1 Cor. 15:12–22; Rev. 21:1–4). The order of worship and the
prayers were taken from the Service of Witness to the Resurrection found
in the *Book of Common Worship* of the Presbyterian Church (U.S.A.). The
purpose, as stated in the sermon, was to provide a model of what the funeral service ought to look and sound like when it is a service of joyful affirmation of Christian hope.

While living in the Boston area, I became fascinated with gravestones of
the late seventeenth and early eighteenth century. The New England Puri-
tans were very cautious about any sanctuary decoration, but their tombstones
were often intricately and elaborately carved. Some carried Latin inscrip-
tions: "memento mori" (remember death) and "fugit hora" (the hours flee)
were the two most popular. Many carried brief poems, often touching, some
verging on the humorous. My favorite goes something like this:

> Look well to me as you pass by,
> As you are now, so once was I.
> As I am now, so you shall be.
> Prepare for death and follow me.

We can learn much about a culture by observing its funeral customs, because there we see what people believe about death and also about life. Today is Memorial Day, and I have learned that for many of you it's still Decoration Day, a day to visit and tend the graves of family and friends. In this congregation, it is our custom to give thanks on this day for all the gifts we have received as memorials to members and friends who have died.

Since this year our observance falls in the season of Eastertide while we are still celebrating our Lord's resurrection, it seemed appropriate this morning to give some thought to the nature of a Christian funeral. Today's service, its order and music, is suggested by our Presbyterian resource book on the funeral. We call the service "a witness to the resurrection." Since I conduct so many funeral services in this church, it seems a good time for me to share with you what I think we are doing when we conduct a funeral—because, as the bit of doggerel verse I quoted suggests, it is important that we prepare for death, our own as well as the deaths of those we love and live with.

At its heart, the Christian funeral is a witness to hope. All that we do in such a service—what we say and most especially the music that we hear and sing—everything should point us, not backward in nostalgia, but forward in hope. Christian faith dares to believe that we face death not in resignation or despair but with confidence, with trust, and with hope. You hear me proclaim this hope at every funeral I conduct: in life and in death we belong to God, and nothing in life or in death can separate us from God's love for us in Christ Jesus our Lord.

At its best a Christian funeral service (and the time surrounding it—the recounting of memories, the gathering of family and friends, the sharing of a meal), all of that should accomplish three things: first, thanksgiving; second, dealing with the pain; and third, bearing witness to the resurrection.

First of all, a Christian funeral is an occasion for thanksgiving. I begin each service by saying: "We are gathered here to worship God and to give thanks to God for the life of . . ." This is more than a set phrase: it announces the tone and nature of the service. We gather to remember and to give thanks. The point of a eulogy is not to assure the immortality of the deceased by recounting his or her good life. The point of words and prayers remembering one who has died is to raise up again the gifts God has given us through that person's life.

No matter the nature of the person or the manner of death, in every life there is something for which we can and should be grateful to God. No matter how long or short, no matter how painful or difficult the life, no matter what the person may have done to injure self or others—in every life there is something which should be remembered with gratitude before God.

The more funerals I conduct, the clearer it is to me how important it is for us to recognize those things in each other's lives and to give thanks *now* while we are still alive. The most difficult regrets I have had to deal with in my own grieving have been my failures to speak my gratitude and love while those loved were still living. You and I do not have forever to tell someone what their life means to us. It *is* important to gather up those feelings at a funeral. It is ever so much more valuable to speak these things to each other in this life.

The first purpose of a funeral is to give thanks. The second is to deal with the pain death inevitably brings. We never experience death without also experiencing some amount of anger, regret, and unresolved feelings. What is unresolved may be simply that you did not get to say goodbye, that you never found that right moment to express your love and gratitude. What is unresolved may be years of pain and deep hurt. It may be that your pain in the relationship was so great that you secretly wanted the person to die, and now you fear that your thoughts may have somehow contributed to the death. Or sometimes death is such a blessed relief after long suffering that you feel guilty about feeling relieved that the waiting is over.

Unresolved feelings come in all sizes and shapes. But the people who have been through grief support groups will tell you how absolutely necessary it is for all of us who grieve to confront and express and work through those feelings. Sometimes a funeral service itself can help this process. A colleague of mine in Austin preached a funeral for a church member who committed suicide. In her meditation, Laura led us through all our feelings: guilt that we hadn't noticed the man's pain; regret that we had not done *something;* anger that he went away and left us with the guilt and regret; helplessness in the face of tragedy.

Sometimes the service can do that, but more often dealing with the pain happens in conversations before and after, often months after. If we are friends and neighbors and companions to those who mourn, our greatest gift is to listen, to let the pain come out, and not to block it with well-meaning platitudes (such as "well, that's in the past, it's time to move on" or "you did all you could do, don't feel bad"). Pain is usually not pretty, but pain that is not dealt with is much worse.

A Christian funeral is an occasion for thanksgiving; it is an opportunity to deal with the pain; it is finally, and most importantly, a witness to the resurrection.

One could say that the purpose of all religion is to help humans deal with the reality, and the inevitability, of death. Some religions answer the problem of death with belief in reincarnation (I don't really die; I come back in another form). Some answer it by belief in the immortality of the soul (the essence of me doesn't die; that is immortal). Some hold to an "objective immortality" (I live on in the memories of my descendants).

Christians believe in *resurrection*. This begins with the conviction that the resurrection of Christ was the beginning and the sign of the new life God promises to all people and all creation. Resurrection is a belief about history before it is a belief about me personally. Resurrection is the end of the biblical story: God created the world and everything good, but when human sin entered creation, everything changed. We became estranged, separated from God, alienated from ourselves, at war with one another. And the whole creation suffered. Because of our sin, death became painful and terrifying, a symbol of ultimate separation from life and God.

But, the story continues, God intends to remake the creation. God intends to overcome the estrangement and separation we have caused. God intends to restore us to right relationship with God, with ourselves, and with one another. That restoration is called "resurrection." In resurrection we receive two promises. To us individually, God promises "eternal life"— that is, life of unbroken union with God. To the whole creation, God promises a new heaven and a new earth, where there is no more pain, no more separation, for the former things have passed away.

There are Christians who have timetables, charts, and maps for how this resurrection, this new creation, will happen. On that subject, I am frankly agnostic: I have no clue about the details. I only trust that God has made a promise that God intends to keep. When asked what all this will be like, I think now I understand Paul's metaphor of the wheat: what we see in our fields is nothing like the grain that is sown. Paul suggests that our life now is like the seed grain, and God's promise, God's new creation, is like the supple, lustrous wheat.

For me the details of resurrection are not important. What is important is the promise that in life and in death we belong to God and that there will be a new creation. I don't know the details, but I do know the One who promises, and so I try with my life to bear witness: a witness to hope.

# 6

# Venerable Preaching

*Joseph R. Jeter, Jr.*

A priest named Zechariah was on duty in the sanctuary when an angel appeared to him and said, "Do not be afraid, your prayers have been heard. Your wife Elizabeth will bear you a son and you shall call his name John." Zechariah said, "How can this be, for I am an old man and my wife is getting on in years?" The angel replied, "I am Gabriel. I stand in the presence of God, and I have been sent to speak to you and to bring you this good news. But now, because you did not believe my words, which will be fulfilled in their time, you will be mute, unable to speak, until the day these things occur" (based on Luke 1:5–20).

Have we got a bone to pick with Gabriel or what? I think Zechariah had a perfectly legitimate question.[1] If Gabriel did not like that question, wait till he hears some of the questions I have. Why are they raping and slaughtering each other in Bosnia, Gabriel? Why are they starving in Somalia? How about Haiti? How about Waco? Tell us and I will gladly shut up. Or do you only silence old people who ask what you think are impertinent questions? When someone once said that we shall have a lot to answer for when we stand before the throne of grace, Carlyle Marney is reputed to have replied, "So shall God." My mother exists today in a nursing home, incontinent, suffering from Alzheimer's, robbed of her dignity, her strength, her mind.[2] And I have a few questions for us preachers in our role as stand-ins for Gabriel. And so do people in our congregations. How will we answer?

Here then is the first question. There are multitudes of books and conferences on "the problem of aging." But whose problem is it? We are all aging; some of us just have a head start on the rest of you. Is the problem primarily one for those who have attained "old age" or for those who have not? This is a question that can perhaps only be answered poetically. Jean-Paul Sartre suggested the problem was one imposed on him by others:

> Everyone treats me as an old man. I laugh about it. Why? Because
> an old man never feels like an old man. I understand from others
> what old age implies for those who see it from without, but I do
> not feel my old age. Thus my old age is not a thing that in itself
> teaches me something. What teaches me something is the attitude
> of others toward me. To put it another way, the fact that I am old
> for others is to be profoundly old. Old age is for me a reality that
> others feel, they see me and say, "This is a nice old man," and they
> are kind because I will die soon, and afterwards they are
> respectful, etc.: it is others who are my old age.[3]

Age has more to do with self-image and relationships than it does with
the chronometer. To say that "old age is a state of mind" is to risk trivial-
ization. But there is something to that maxim. Witness these lines from the
lovely poem "Evening Train," by Denise Levertov:

> An old man sleeping in the evening train,
> face upturned, mouth discreetly closed,
> hands clasped, with fingers interlaced. . . .
> How tired he is, how tired.
> I called him old, but then I remember . . .
> [that] in that dimension
> that moves with us but keeps itself still
> like the bubble in a carpenter's level . . .
> Everyone has an unchanging age (or sometimes two)
> carried with them, beyond expression.
> This man perhaps
> is ten, putting in a few hours most days
> in a crowded schoolroom, and a lot more
> at work in the fields; a boy who's always
> making plans to go fishing his first free day.
> The train moves through the dark quite swiftly . . .
> with its load of people, each . . .
> with a known age and that other,
> the hidden one . . . not a point of arrest but a core
> around which the mind develops, reflections circle,
> events accrue—a center.[4]

So whose problem is old age? Everyone's. What has been said of Martin
Luther, that "he lived between two ages," is true of all of us. If we carry
within us a hidden age that marks our center, and without us another age,
thrust upon us by time and other people, then the maintenance of a functional, creative equilibrium "between ages" becomes a task for everyone. A
good self-image and good relationships with others are crucial to that task.
Can preachers be of help? We shall see.

### Aging and Preaching:
### A Historical Sketch

I have been asked to address the question of preaching by and to older adults, to look for clues in Christian history on this matter, and to offer methodological suggestions, should I have any. To begin with, there is little in standard homiletical histories and texts about this question. Why? Obviously, prior to the twentieth century, preaching to older persons was not seen to be an issue or a problem. Why?

In the first place, there were not that many older persons in days of yore. In the early and medieval times, when few lived past forty, preaching to what might today be considered older persons was not an issue. Second, while aged persons might have presented a problem individually, they did not present a problem as a class.[5] Older persons, especially the frail and infirm, were cared for by their families. While old Johannes or Tabitha might have presented a problem because of the care required, older persons in general did not. At least that is the standard line. My tendency is to doubt that somewhat, to suspect that many older persons were neglected or badly treated, and died before their time. But I have no information about that to share.

What *do* we know? In the Hebrew Bible we find older adults very much a part of the family and the community. The aged Abraham and Sarah were active and vital, progenitors of the faith and the faithful. We are happy for them, as we are saddened by the fact that old Moses, after leading that grievance committee for forty years in the wilderness, does not get to enter the land of promise. We are hampered, when speaking of the New Testament, by the fact that Jesus never specifically addressed the question of aging.[6] Paul's contribution was a clear distinction between flesh and spirit, with spirit more to be desired than flesh, an affirmation often used to comfort those whose flesh is failing. In the early church there consequently existed a genuine respect for older persons, a concern with the necessary assistance needed by them, and the suggestion that older persons of mature faith were particularly effective in performing the "spiritual ministries" of the church: counseling, prayer, and so forth.[7] This attractive picture, however factual, was not to last.

A creeping morbidity overlay large chunks of medieval history, one which affected preaching as well as other facets of culture. Life was a sad story from cradle to grave, and old age did not escape the tragedy. G. R. Owst, examining a number of medieval sermons, relates their descriptions of old age in this way: "They all tell eloquently of the wrinkled face, the hoar head, the bent back, the failing sight, hearing, limbs, the livid nose and nails, the evil breath, the hollow eye."[8] This approach culminated in Shakespeare's *As You Like It*, where the scene introduced by the famous line, "All the world's a stage," suggests that there are "seven ages of man"—infant, schoolboy, lover, soldier, justice, what we might call decline, and finally:

> Last scene of all,
> That ends this strange eventful history,
> Is second childishness and mere oblivion,
> Sans teeth, sans eyes, sans taste, sans everything.[9]

These extremely negative views, though they still endure, must be balanced with more charitable views, harkening back to the days of reverencing the old and looking forward to the days when people would live longer, better.

Life for older adults in colonial America was actually closer to the stories we read in the Hebrew Bible than to life today. Carole Haber suggests that old age is today marked by sharp boundaries, often called "role exits": work has ended; children are grown, married, departed. To the contrary, she says, in the eighteenth century (and, I would suggest, much earlier) "old age was often a more ambiguous stage of existence. The boundary separating it from maturity was less explicit and segmented."[10] Such libraries as there were in colonial America would not have had shelves laden with books on "aging." "Retirement" as a phenomenon had not yet even been invented.

Sermons on old age remaining from the nineteenth century tend to romanticize aging, as in one by Frederick Hastings in 1885, who suggested in a three-point sermon based on Acts 21:16 that "with increasing years should come an increasing delight in learning of Christ," that "with added years should come increasing desire to be helpful to others," and finally that, with old age, come "hints of immortality."[11]

It seems a great distance from veneration of the aged as "holy ones" of God to today's frequent description of older persons as those who suffer from isolation, depression, and loss of independence, self-esteem, work, and time.[12] But we have traveled that distance almost unconsciously, especially when it comes to preaching. The most famous book on preaching, at least in this country, was John Broadus's 1870 book *On the Preparation and Delivery of Sermons.* His advice on preaching to older persons comes in a couple of sentences. "The pastor may sometimes wish to preach especially to the aged. It is not necessary to discuss the best ways of preaching to them . . . as always—preach the gospel."[13] More recently, Paul Maves and J. Lennart Cedarleaf's study, *Older People and the Church,* laments:

> It has not proved possible for us to study the extent to which aging
> and older persons are referred to in contemporary sermons. Our
> general impression is that only rarely is there even an oblique

reference to aging, and even then euphemisms are likely to be used.[14]

In the face of this blithe and benign (one hopes) neglect of older adults in the history of preaching, Russell Mase writes that today's preacher

> faces an enormous task of dissociating the hearers' conception of their self-worth from the engulfing tide of advertising, literature, media representations, and all the rest of the massive assault on the elderly by a culture that equates old with bad, aging with loss of status and worth, illness and disability with depreciation of life value, and death, finally, with non-being.[15]

In other historical studies I have consulted, I have found much on prayer and music for older persons, nothing on preaching. There remains much work to be done here. And with that admission, we now turn to the present question of "venerable" preaching, looking at it from both sides of the pulpit.

## Older Preachers

One day in graduate school we were sitting in class jabbering about how we wanted to be addressed when we got out of school: Pastor this, Reverend that, Brother or Sister So-and-so. Our dear professor broke in to say, "The one I'm bucking for is 'The Venerable.'" That put an end to our pretension that day and makes a beginning for us on this day. With the exception of the Venerable Bede, there are very few instances in the West (unlike the East) where this title has been bestowed upon a scholar or cleric. And is it really a title that we would want to buck for? If a minister came to be known in church circles as "The Venerable Smith," could he or she get a call from a congregation?

Looking at the question of venerable preaching from the preacher's side of the pulpit, we have fewer persons today preaching into their seventies and beyond. It did not use to be that way. One of the precious traditions of the church is that of the elder John being carried to the pulpit where he would address his people: "Little children, love one another." And many of us can remember from our youth those white-haired veterans of the cross who led us to the throne of grace. I was baptized and led to ministry by a preacher in his eighties. But this is rare now. Whether it is the changing shape of ministry that turns us gladly out to pasture at sixty-five, sometimes discouraged and burned out, or whether it is the changing expectations of people in a fast-moving world who want a young, up-to-date preacher, there are fewer venerable preachers around.

Of course, there are some older brothers and sisters just hitting their stride as their contemporaries retire and doing the best preaching of their life, and there are some who are still preaching who should not be. There is something to be said for dying in the pulpit. (Literally, I mean. All of us have figuratively died a thousand deaths there.) But it does not always work out that way. And there is, for many of us, a time to stop and step down. How does one know? We preachers need some honest friends who will tell us. And we need to listen and move on to the other challenges God will set before us. In response to the problem of "role exits" previously mentioned, G. H. Asquith Jr. suggests, in words appropriate to both those who preach and those who listen to the preaching:

> A spiritual task for the older person is to reframe the sense of self apart from the work role. In a society replete with "works theology," this involves a personal integration of the fundamental meaning of justification by faith—the acceptance of self, others, and God for who one *is* rather than for what one *does*. Vocation can then be seen as the appropriate, focused investment of one's life energy in contrast to simply one's paid occupation.[16]

In a time when more and more people are changing careers and outliving their careers, including preachers, the re-visioning of Christian vocation must be an important theme of the pulpit.

## Older Listeners:
## Memory and Hope

Now let us move to the other side of the pulpit. How does one of whatever age preach *to* and *for* the venerable, to and for the saints of God gathered before us, most of whom are healthy and well? Studies have shown that upward of a third of the members of mainline churches are now over sixty-five, and many of us have served congregations where the average age was higher than that. Is there anything we should do differently? I think so.

While I agree with the Christian tradition that suggests that aging is a part of life and therefore not to be treated differently, that the aging are not to be set apart from the community and addressed only about their particular concerns, I do think there are some things preachers can learn that will make their preaching more effective to all groups, including elders. There are certain tensions involved in preaching, along with the rest of our ministry, that impact older adults particularly hard, and I would like to address two of them.

The first has to do with *memory*. In an essay on worship and aging, Urban T. Holmes suggests that worship is an act of memory and, more radically, that "a person with no memory is one incapable of worship."[17] Older adults have a rich storehouse of memories and stories. But often it is this part of the body of Christ whose stories are ignored in sermons or, worse, stereotyped in a negative way.

In 1987 I participated in a conference sponsored by the American Association of Retired Persons on the question of preaching to older adults. In a paper for the conference Clyde Fant wrote:

> The sermon is affected little by whether the congregation is old or young. . . . However, there may be one vital exception. The importance of the stories of the old should not be overlooked. The preacher must be involved in learning and sharing these stories.[18]

How can this work? I remember one occasion when my father and I were in church. The preacher was going on, and my father sat, apparently uninterested. The preacher then happened to mention something that had happened to him growing up on the farm. One of his chores, after the chickens had gone to roost on the rain barrel, was to pick them up and gently turn them so they faced inward. My father began to smile and then chuckle and then belly laugh. I looked at him. What was going on? I didn't find the story particularly engaging. But my father did. It brought back memories of his days on the farm when he had done exactly the same thing. It was a part of his experience. And captured by the image and the connections the preacher made, my father was much more engaged with the rest of the sermon. Tapping into the memories and stories of elders is a rich resource for our sermons and those who listen to them. Reminiscence has been found to have considerable value in community bonding and building.[19]

Let me tell you about Margaret LaHorgue. When I became the pastor of the little Christian Church in Upland, California, I set out to call on the folk. The secretary provided me with a list of the leaders that I should see first off. But I just took the membership directory, opened it, picked a name, and went knocking on her door. Margaret opened the door and I identified myself as the new preacher. I recognized her as a little woman who sat quietly toward the back of the church. She let me in, we sat down, and she began to cry. I didn't know what I had done wrong and asked her, "What's the matter?" She finally said, "I've been a member of this church since 1940 and you're the first minister who's ever come to see me." I took her hand and said, "Well, I'm here now." And we began to visit. She told me her story, how she had come over from Spain in 1912 with her family. We were soon down on the floor with the old albums out, looking at the pictures. There was one of her family, taken shortly after they arrived: Papa, with the big mustache, seated; Mama at his shoulder; the children arrayed around them; Margaret, fifteen then, there on the end. I stared in amazement and finally looked up at her. She smiled at me and said, "I was pretty then, wasn't I?" Well, pretty wasn't nearly enough of a word to describe that beautiful young woman in the photograph, and I said, truly, "Yes, you were very beautiful, and you still are." Margaret LaHorgue became my right-hand woman in that church, always ready to help me any way she could. All because I took time to hear her story. And though long since gone, Margaret is now part of the memory that I will carry into my old age, a memory that I am happy to share with you.

The other pole of this tension is tunnel vision. Ignoring the stories and memories of elder persons is a great waste. Focusing upon them alone is a distortion of our faith, which is most fully vested in the future. As Holmes puts it: "The wisdom that graces the older person can be defined as the willingness to acknowledge what the past has made us and yet forgive the past that we might be open to the future."[20] Living in his eighth decade, Richard Crews never fails to remind me when he sees me struggling, "Joey, it gets better." And another septuagenarian told me last week when I spoke with him about this subject, "Tell them I don't want to hear sermons which address only the toothless reminiscences of old age. Aging is a part of our lives, not the whole. I come to church to remember, because that propels me forward, not to reminisce, because that pulls me back." Most older folk that I work with tell me they appreciate the respect that is shown by taking their stories seriously, they appreciate how that includes them within the body. They do not appreciate being either invisible or the sole focus of attention. Sartre (quoted at the beginning of this chapter) has shown us the problem with that.

Now let me say a word about *hope*, which also has particular relevance for older adults. Day before yesterday was the first Sunday in Lent. I meet each week with a group of preachers who have a lectionary study group. Sunday's texts were the temptation stories from the Garden of Eden and Jesus in the wilderness. But these preachers, to my surprise and joy, chose to preach on the psalm for the day. Psalm 130 is one of the traditional seven penitential psalms. It deals not so much with concepts as with feelings. It is the song of one who has hit bottom, rock bottom, "Out of the depths I cry to thee"; one who feels unworthy, "If you should mark our iniquities, Lord, who could stand?" but one who affirms the forgiveness of God, "There is forgiveness with you." This is followed by a touching pair of couplets in verses 5 and 6:

> I wait for the Lord, my soul waits,
>     and in God's word I hope.
> My soul waits for the Lord
>     more than those who watch for the morning,
>     more than those who watch for the morning.

Older people, perhaps more than any other segment of our congregations, feel the burden of time that the psalmist sings about, imaged powerfully as a sleepless night. The repetition gives us the feeling of how time can drag:

> More than those who watch for the morning,
> More than those who watch for the morning.

Many older adults spend a disproportionate amount of their time waiting: waiting to see the doctor, waiting for someone, anyone, to walk in the room at the nursing home, waiting for the telephone to ring, waiting for morning to come. But look at what the psalm says. Waiting equals hope. This is not necessarily a joyous waiting, but it's a sure and confident one. "My soul waits for the Lord" and "in God's word I hope." They are the same thing.[21] Much of life reduces more than anything else to waiting. And if preachers can address the creative, hopeful potential inherent in waiting, a real service can be performed for older and younger persons alike.

So where is the tension here? I mentioned the Venerable Bede earlier. One of the memorable stories about this eighth-century theologian has him, advanced in years and in poor health, still at work translating the Gospel of John into Anglo-Saxon. He was lying on his pallet in the monastery dictating his translation to a young monk. As he neared the end of the Gospel, he turned to the monk and said, "Write fast." He then gave him the last few lines of the Gospel, closed his eyes, and breathed his last.[22]

The other side of waiting is hurrying. During his last illness, when Nikos Kazantzakis still had so much more he wanted to say, he told his wife that he wished he could go down to the streetcorner with a begging bowl and cry out to the passersby: "Alms, friends, a quarter-hour of your time."[23] There are those who have nothing to do and feel useless. There are those who have much to do and feel frustrated by the merciless ticking of the clock. As one old scholar says in Trevanian's *The Summer of Katya*:

> For me time is sand sifting through my fingers. Not enough of it. Can't seem to grasp hold of it. While for my son, time is a heavy burden of boredom around his neck, something to be got rid of, something to be got through.[24]

The message of the monks that we focus on each day's task and leave the rest to God is good meat for homiletical treatment. In words I have heard attributed to Reinhold Niebuhr, "Anything worth doing well cannot be completed in one lifetime." Sometimes the sermon is patience. Sometimes the sermon is "write fast." And we need to hear them both, because both are real. Our elder brothers and sisters are pilgrim people. They are people of adventure, who seek new experiences and look forward to tomorrow.[25] When the dragging or racing of time becomes a burden, the good news needs to be preached that our time, like the rest of our lives, is in the hands of God. In the fullness of time, scripture says, God came to us. But not just in the fullness. In the shortness and the heaviness as well.

## Conclusions

Two central ingredients to an effective preaching ministry with older adults are those of memory and hope, a ministry that honors and puts to work these two rich blessings of our elders. And how shall we deal with the tension that inevitably surrounds these blessings? Dietrich Ritschl has an interesting answer. He went so far as to call his study of Jesus Christ exactly what we have been talking about: *Memory and Hope*. And he has this to say:

> The Church's recognition of [the presence of Christ] enables [us] to "hope backward," i.e., that [Jesus Christ] may change and remove those elements of the past which still burden the present and destroy the hope for the future, and to "remember forward," i.e., that the promises of the past may be fulfilled in the future.[26]

I like that and what it may also say about an effective homiletical approach to aging. Good preaching to our elders is one which calls them to "remember forward," to make of their shared and individual memories the stuff upon which a future can be built for the church, and to "hope backward," to realize that their hope, like ours, does not rest in the losses of age, but in the gains won for us by Jesus Christ.

At the beginning of this lecture I mentioned my mother, who has been in a nursing home for almost a year now, and the questions her suffering and ours have raised in me. I need also to tell you about Thanksgiving. As it approached, my father suggested the possibility of my mother coming to our house for Thanksgiving dinner, to which we would invite her brother and sister-in-law as well. Mother's brother also has Alzheimer's and this would probably be the last time they would see each other.[27] I was nervous. The doctor advised against it, saying that Alzheimer's patients often do not do well outside their familiar environment. But I went ahead. Dad took mother's best clothes and her jewelry over and, with the help of the staff, dressed her and put on her makeup. Before they brought her over, they walked up and down the halls so everyone could see how pretty she looked! (There is a community in nursing homes which allows the folk to rejoice in the small victories of one another!) I went to Euless to get Uncle Jack and his wife and brought them over. Then came the critical moment. Would they recognize each other? Well, Jack and Mama met in front of the fireplace and they hugged each other for a long time. Finally, my uncle said, "We had some times, didn't we, kid?" And in a moment of perfect lucidity,

my mother looked up at him and said, "Yes, we sure did." I will never forget that moment and I am so grateful for it. They were "remembered forward" into clarity by those old times and can "hope backward" in the days
ahead.[28] The foundation of faith in such situations, firmly rooted in both
scripture and tradition, is found in the words of Denise Dombkowski Hopkins: "God will remember, even as the patient with Alzheimer's slowly for-
gets."[29]

Two additional themes were suggested for this chapter that I have not
addressed. First is the question of whether or not preaching approaches
should take into account different senior age sets—fifty-five to sixty-five,
sixty-five to seventy-five, and seventy-five and beyond. I am aware of current tendencies to differentiate among smaller age groups, but I have little
to add and would be shooting in the dark on that, so I will not.

Second, what forms, styles, and approaches are most likely to be well received and effective with older persons? I am being led here, I suspect, to
suggest that the so-called "newer" methods (inductive, narrative, story, and
so forth) are less effective and that we need to use the old familiar deductive and expository approaches. But I am not willing to do or say that. My
experience, quite frankly, when I have brought new ideas and methods to
churches and groups, is that the older people are more open to being
stretched than the younger people are. When I spoke to a group of Christian men in Ohio some time back concerning my ideas about the book of
Revelation, the older men were attentive and engaging. The younger men
thought I was a heretic and would not listen.

There is a specific setting where traditional methods seem to work best
and that is the nursing home or convalescent center. Preaching to institutionalized older people brings with it certain problems that are not preva-
lent in the church congregation: (1) The dynamics of a multigenerational
audience are changed. The "slang of the moment" may not be heard in
quite the same way it is in a local congregation. (2) There may be only one
service available to people of different faiths, which may or may not respect
the integrity of their own beliefs. (3) Worship is often conducted by various clergy on a rotating basis. This mean there is little, if any, continuity
in preaching. (4) Because some clergy perform this task grudgingly, they
are often poorly prepared. (5) Many such guest clergy, especially the
young, seem to think that what older people really want to hear is a message on the meaning of death. This generally is more a problem of the minister who may be struggling with his or her own mortality than it is that of
the audience, who by and large have come to terms with the question. Sermons on life and its meaning are more needed. (6) Many institutionalized
persons have physical limitations that the preacher must take into account.
The need to speak clearly and to project one's voice is especially important
for a group of people who may have various levels of hearing impairment.

Also the "prophetic" charge to "go out and do something" may be painful to those who cannot go out. Calls to action need to be realistic and helpful, not hopeless or guilt-producing.[30]

To these caveats let me add that preaching in institutional settings has been a very positive experience for me. I have found these elders to be most appreciative and affirming listeners. Solid biblical or doctrinal preaching always finds a willing audience. Sermons about relationships are heard in their immediacy. Such preaching occasions are among my fondest memories.

The last lines of Cicero's magnificent dialogue *On Old Age* are as wise and delightful now as they were two thousand years ago: "That is what I think about old age. May you live to see the condition. Then you will be able to prove by experience that what I have told you is true."[31]

**SERMON**

# Clasping Hands across the Years

Joseph R. Jeter, Jr.

*Occasion for sermon:* This sermon has lived through several incarnations, having been preached mostly to seminarians and seniors, who have a number of things in common. They live on the margins of the culture, have everyone telling them who to be and what to do, and face together the danger that comes from handling holy things too many times. In the face of that, they remain faithful, hopeful, and loving. They are my favorite audiences.

One generation shall laud thy works to another.

Ps. 145:4

Consider the handshake. Inferior to the hug. But not bad. It is close. In fact, it is as close as some of us will ever get. Sure, it has its problems. There are some macho men out there who do not feel that they have really shaken your hand until they have fractured your metacarpals. On election night in 1960, when the news came that Ohio had gone for Nixon, John F. Kennedy held up his raw, puffy, battered hand and said, "Ohio did that to me."[1] In some cultures a handshake means nothing.[2] But in the culture in which I was raised, it was more important than a contract. Shaking hands can indicate good will and peace, an end to hostilities, or binding agreement, but the most important thing we do when we shake hands is simply to acknowledge and affirm each other's presence. "Here am I. Here are you. Here we are." And it is not always easy to do that. Fred Craddock, America's finest preacher, was so shy when he was young that he remembers being twenty-two years of age the first time he could muster up the gumption to put out his hand and say "Hello, my name's Fred Craddock."[3]

I want us to consider this sense of presence today as we look both to the past and the future. The past is closer than we think. British poet Richard Aldington once said that he knew he was a real poet, because he was only four handshakes away from Shelley.[4] And he had proof. He had once shaken hands with the poet Swinburne, who had shaken hands with Southey, who had shaken hands with Walter Savage Landor, who was a close friend of Shelley. Just four handshakes away. That is close! And I like it! You see, I have shaken hands with William Jackson Jarman, who shook hands with George Hamilton Combs, who shook hands with Alexander Procter, who shook hands with Alexander Campbell, the great man himself. I am just four handshakes away from Campbell, which makes the founder of my denomination seem closer than he was before.

You see how it works? Halford Luccock points out that anyone who has shaken hands with an ordained Methodist minister (and who has not?) can truly say that he or she is only six handshakes away from John Wesley. Just six. And we could go on. We are only seven handshakes away from Thomas Jefferson, nine away from Anne Hutchinson, thirteen away from Martin Luther, and about sixteen away from Joan of Arc. That is not very far. Wie geht es ihnen! Bonjour! Close . . . very close.

But . . . we know better. Our text for this morning says that God is great, and that one generation shall laud God's works to another. In our happier moments, we are like the psalmist who composed this, one of only two psalms that bear the title, a psalm of praise. We sense that there is meaning in continuity, that memory begets hope, that what we have received from others, we, like Paul, deliver to those who come after us, continuing to laud the works of God from one generation to another.

However, in the cold gray light of morning, we realize that it is not always like that. As we get older, sometimes memory and hope get disconnected, and the distance between past and future lengthens like the shadows of evening. We worry about the future, that the next generation has not heard the message they will need to live as God's people, and we fear that we may not have done a good enough job in delivering that message. Many complaints about young people are really rhetorical questions about our own success or failure as bearers of the faith.

I think of my son. How much more difficult is the road he and his peers must walk than the one I walked thirty-five years ago. We were not faced with drugs, gangs, or AIDS. Television was a novelty, not our principal educator. And we did not live in a time of rampant cynicism about the institutions of our society. How will he do? How have I done? Have I, have we, effectively lauded God's works to his generation? Time will tell.

Just as we fear a break between the present and the future, we also have the nagging fear that there is a growing disjuncture between us and the past, between us and the great saints and reformers who shaped the institutions we love so well. Somewhere along the line, something got lost, a handshake did not take, the line got broken, and we are left serving up strange fire before Jehovah. We sometimes feel less like the psalmist and more like Second Isaiah, who said: "Let the people assemble. Who among them can declare this? Who can show us the former ways?" (43:9). Our memories, which we thought were our strong suit, have become as short as our vision. We can feel cut off from our moorings in both past and future and lapse into discouragement and depression.

What is it, friends, that is lacking in us, that keeps us from effectively declaring the former things and lauding the works of God for as long as we live? What is it that separates us from the saints and witnesses? Why do we sing their praises with hollow voices, recalling but not remembering?

Why? Is it that we are not as dedicated as those of old, who never gave up hope? I do not believe that. In my life and ministry I have seen such dedication. I have seen people ready to reach, to extend, to risk everything. The long list of martyrs to the faith increases in our day. I remember a phone call that I received in 1964 from a friend in Mississippi. The Klan and the sheriff were banging at the door and he just wanted to tell me that he loved me in case we did not see each other again. There are people like Oscar Romero, like Rosa Parks, like my brother minister Marvin Kennon, who laid his body across the entrance to the Livermore Lab in California with the words, "O Christ" upon his lips. I remember a dear woman named Faye Goostree. She was distressed that so many elderly people were malnourished in our community. She knocked on official door after official door, only to be told that nothing could be done. Then she began working on the pastors. They hemmed and hawed and finally gave in to her persistence and Meals on Wheels in Fort Worth became a reality. Wherever there is injustice, there are people who stand against it. Whenever there is suffering, there are people willing to share the pain. No, our alienation from the saints is not one of indifference or lack of dedication.

Is it that we do not know the Bible? I do not believe that, either. I hear it all the time, but I do not believe it. We know more about Paul than Paul did. We know the Bible. If there is a problem here, it is that our biblical skills are those of the coroner and not the obstetrician—doing autopsies, not assisting birth. But our alienation from the saints is not one of knowledge.

Is it that we have lost a clear moral and theological posture? Some people think so. I do not. Our theology and our ethics are where they have always been: in process and in agony. In the fourth century Gregory of Nyssa lamented:

> If you ask anyone in Constantinople for change, he will start
> discussing whether the Son is begotten or unbegotten. If you ask
> about the quality of bread, you will get the answer: "The Father is
> more; the Son is less." If you suggest taking a bath, you will be
> told, "There was nothing before the Son was created."[5]

So what else is new . . . or old. The quest for the true and the good goes
on, with as diligent searchers, I am convinced, as we have ever had. Final
understanding always exceeds our grasp, but our partial understanding has
never been better and is not what separates us from the saints.

I do not believe that our distance from the saints may be laid primarily
at the feet of our lack of dedication, knowledge, or understanding. Let me
risk suggesting two things that may be a problem, two factors that can separate us from those who have gone before and who will go beyond—one
personal, one corporate. In the first place, many of us have come to neglect
the spiritual side of our faith. Put bluntly, we have lost touch with Jesus. I
have a friend, a good pastor, who struggled with this for years and then finally said, in a half-joking manner, that he had given up his devotional life
for Lent. He said it had really freed him up—no more guilt about not praying enough, no more backaches from sitting still trying to meditate. On the
other hand, he said, "I have to accept that whatever power I have comes
from what I do and not who I am. And that hurts." Yes, it does.

The great preacher James Stewart wrote:

> Our basic need . . . is a rediscovery of Christianity as *a vital
> relationship to a living Christ.* . . . The longer one lives and the more
> deeply one ponders the human dilemma, the clearer does this
> become. . . . If, as Christians, we hope to grow in grace and walk
> the way of faith and hope and love, the prior condition is that our
> own life should be intertwined with that of Jesus.[6]

What kind of difference can this make? Listen to this. W. Carl Ketcher-
side was described as a "wing commander" of the anti-instrumental, anti-
college Sommerite Church of Christ[7] (which says something about the zoo
of American denominationalism). For thirty years he fought sectarian battles, preached a narrow, legalistic gospel, scored as a champion debater and
an editor-bishop, built hundreds of churches and baptized thousands of
people. Then, while on a mission to Ireland, he fell into utter despair and
uncertainty. One wintry night in a little frame chapel, alone and cold and
feeling very old, he was meditating on Rev. 3:20, when he did what he had
never done before during his long years of religious warfare: he invited Jesus
into his heart. "Behold, I stand at the door and knock. If anyone hears my
voice and opens the door, I will come in . . ." The remaining years of Ketch-
erside's ministry were very different from those which had gone before.[8]

The older we become, the more we have handled sacred things along the way. Familiarity may breed contempt. And the danger there is that the mystery and wonder dissolve before us and leave us with a secondhand faith. One seldom lauds a secondhand faith to the next generation. Why bother? All our dedication, knowledge, and understanding do not replace our need for presence, for contact. When we give up on that quest for contact between ourselves and the living Christ, lose hope of ever shaking hands with the Eternal Now, we cut ourselves off from the spring at which the saints drank so deeply.

The other thing that may keep us from participating in the praise of the psalmist is the gradual loss of faith in the church as the instrument of the will of God. This rarely happens overnight, but instead, slowly, insidiously. The church seems to change. It is not what it used to be, and we question the direction in which it seems to be moving. Almost everyone, young and old alike, approaches the church today with greatly lowered expectations. For today's world the church is a kind of dear sleepy anachronism which, even when it cries out from time to time, is easy to pacify with anesthetic god-talk. We remember fondly the church of our youth, which nurtured us in the faith, and we think it could be useful and powerful again, but no one seems to be paying any attention. Remember Father Mulcahy on the TV series *M\*A\*S\*H*? Everyone loved him; he was such a sweet little man. But did you ever notice that he almost never got the good lines, the important lines, the pivotal lines. He was always at the edges and never at the center of the story. I remember reading a letter from a real chaplain. He said, "I am always expected to attend the officers' parties, but I am also expected to leave before the liquor is brought out."[9]

The principalities and powers are on the move today. And the church seems helpless to do anything about it. But, lest we forget, Leslie Weatherhead reminds us that because the church is ordained of God, the one thing it cannot do is fail. As he put it, "It does not matter if you destroy all the copies of a snapshot that have been printed, so long as the negative is in safe hands."[10] I can fail. You can fail. But God's church, in heaven and on earth, ultimately cannot. And William Stringfellow reminds us the principalities and powers will never have the gifts that God gave the church: gifts like discernment, charisma, healing, vigilance, and consolation.[11] We need to reclaim the gifts we opened, played with, and tossed aside like an unwanted toy. We need to stop bemoaning the church's ineffectiveness and boldly proclaim the power we have, made perfect in our weakness by the power of Christ. And we need to remember that the church *will* do what God has ordained for the church to do. We can help or hinder this process by our faith or faithlessness, but we cannot stop it.

Listen to this story. The year 387 C.E. was a lot like this one. People were cantankerous and complaining about the government. In February of that year Emperor Theodosius I imposed a new tax on the people of Antioch. A riot broke out in protest, which culminated in the statues of the emperor and his family being pulled down and dragged through the streets. Almost at once, the anger was replaced by fear, for these insurrectionary acts were punishable by death. Theodosius was furious and vowed to level the city. Old Bishop Flavian hurried off to Constantinople to plead with the emperor. Quaking with fear, the people rushed to the church, where the young preacher left behind by the bishop began preaching and preached every day for twenty-one days. The preacher, named John, remarked that it was interesting that everybody, now that danger had overtaken them, passed by those who were in power, those surrounded by wealth, those who had influence with the emperor, and fled to the church![12]

It *was* the church, through the efforts of Flavian and John, that found a way to solve the crisis and save the city. In his last sermon of the crisis, John, later called Chrysostom, the "golden mouth," closed with these words:

> Declare ye to your children; and let your children tell their children; and their children again another generation. So that all who shall be hereafter, even to the consummation, learning of this act of God's lovingkindness, may call us blessed . . . and may themselves be profited, being stimulated to piety by means of all which has happened. For the history of what has lately happened to us, will have power to profit not only ourselves, if we constantly remember it, but also those who shall come after us.[13]

I tell you this story not just because it is a ringing affirmation of our text, but also because one or two of you may have forgotten what happened in Antioch in 387, although it is only about forty handshakes away. God's memory is longer than ours and God's expectations for the church have not been lowered. In the end, Chrysostom could not prevent the collapse of the empire and the fall of darkness upon the civilization of his time. But he tried. Maybe we cannot prevent it either. But God forgive us if we do not try! If we do not use all the gifts God has given the church to hold a flaming candle against the darkness.

When you feel uncertain about the future, cut off from the familiar ground of the past, and confused about the present, know that there are many, many who are with you. And some of them may be looking to you for help, because they trust you. So stretch out one hand toward the Christ and the other to your neighbor. Stand with courage in Christ's church. Keep the handshakes going. It is not far to a brighter and fairer tomorrow. We are really very close. And there is one more bit of good news. There is still time. Amen.

# 7

# Preaching to Sustain
# Those Who Nurtured Us:
# With Appreciation and Advocacy

*James Earl Massey*

Many of those who look to us for ministry, indeed, an increasingly larger group of persons each year, have lived far longer than they ever thought they would. With respect to age, living longer, they have been surprised by life. This longer life in our time is in part a blessing from the many medical advances that have defeated previously triumphant diseases and sapping ills, like diphtheria, smallpox, and tuberculosis, to name but a few. In addition, far more is now known about childhood diseases, and that knowledge has helped physicians to save more children who live to see not only adulthood but advanced years.

The "senior set," as we might call them, are no small group in our time. You are familiar with the statistics. There are indeed many who like the psalmist can say, "I have been young, and now am old" (Ps. 37:25). This statement of fact is not always spoken, however, in the same spirit of praise to God that the psalmist registered. On the lips of some seniors it is a statement loaded with lament, largely because the surprise of living longer has occasioned some problems that sadden their spirit, and some experiences that make demands upon them that they feel inadequate to handle. The surprises of life are not all good ones, and managing the saddening surprises is not always easy. Concerned, strategic preaching can be of help to persons at such a point in their lives; it can grant supportive, sustaining benefits, helping seniors to deal with circumstances and happenings that are unavoidable and unlikely to be reversed. The aging process, with all of its attendant factors and results, is a case in point.

## I

There are four areas of concern among seniors to which our preaching can be appealingly addressed, but before I focus attention on them I want to share a brief word about the age factor as viewed in the Christian scriptures. It is a word that I believe will grant needed perspective by which human aging can be viewed in a clearer light.

I begin with this: according to the earliest accounts in scripture about human life, the ancestors of the Hebrew people lived about ten to twelve times longer than most people of our day. In Genesis 5, a list appears of some notables whose life span is mentioned. The list is somewhat selective: no women are mentioned, and even Cain, though named in an earlier chapter, receives no further mention here. Interestingly, the first persons on the list lived longer than those who came later in the family line. According to the Genesis 5 report, life surprised Adam with 930 years before he died, and Methuselah, one of his later descendants, lived to be 969 years old. The life spans from Adam down to Noah lasted 700 to 1,000 years; the next humans listed had a successively shorter age and expectancy of time to live. According to other biblical accounts, later patriarchs lived between 100 and 120 years, as Gen. 6:3 appears to predict, but by the time of David and the united monarchy, people were living a paltry 70 to 80 years, as Ps. 90:10 reflects.

The chronicler responsible for the story of the Hebrews has strongly suggested that the human life span shortened as human problems and human evil multiplied in the world. The biblical accounts do show a severely reduced longevity when later age ranges are contrasted with the earliest life spans reported for our ancestors.

Some readers of Genesis have questioned whether those stated ages of the listed Hebrew ancients should be understood as accurate reports. Some of those readers are aware of an apparent similarity between this list and that of the antediluvian Sumerian kings who were credited with exceptionally long lives—nine of whom reigned, in succession, longer than 60,000 years, a quite astronomically high number![1] But a far different perspective and emphasis are before us in Genesis 5, namely the extent to which human sin and multiplied evil tainted and ruined human life, even cutting short the human life span.

As for the possible accuracy of those listed life spans as actual time, I was encouraged in my trust of the account by a news item published some years ago about the death of one Shirali Mislimov, a Russian herdsman in Barzava, Russia, who died at 168 years of age. At the time of death, Mr. Mislimov left a widow, his third wife, who was herself 107, and grandchildren, one of whom was over 100 years old. There were 219 other family members, but we were not told just how many of them were his own children.[2] With such contemporary records available for our study, I have remained open to accept the human life spans reported in Genesis 5 as actual personal time. After all, that account reports the earliest history of the family of Adam, a group benefiting from the vital life force in ways we should expect among humans when life was still young on this planet!

But life here is no longer young, and neither are many who look to us for help in facing what has become wearisome, puzzling, and problematic as they seek to persist, survive, and succeed as persons.

## II

Our preaching can help the aged handle the lingering and sometimes searing pain that results from generations that are disjunctured. Given the personal and social problems of our times, family closeness can no longer be taken for granted, and "respect for one's elders" is increasingly rare in society. Even the advertisers now favor the younger set. Those who nurtured us are not always blessed by nearness of younger, caring persons, even in their times of need. The generations have suffered a grave and traumatic separation.

Consider it! The many changes the elderly have witnessed and survived form a staggering list. Since those who are elderly were born, the world has seen the development of television, frozen foods, plastics, credit cards, atomic fission, air conditioners, pantyhose, radar, fast foods, day-care centers, FM radio, electronic typewriters, computers, and condominiums. Or as a radio commentator poignantly voiced it, there were those days when "time sharing meant togetherness . . . not computers or condominiums," a time when "a chip meant a piece of wood. Hardware meant hardware, and software wasn't even a word." The elderly remember when there were "five and dime" stores, places where things could be bought for five and ten cents! But now? No wonder many among the elderly feel so disjunctured.

We who preach can help them manage the pain of such changes. We can do so by underscoring the importance of human togetherness and by giving renewed attention to family meanings. We can do so by encouraging respect for our elders; after all, they are the ones on whose shoulders we stand, they are those whose prior work has enabled us to reach higher than would have been possible without them. A part of our role as preachers is educating for nurture, which involves us in not only a didactic but a prophetic task.

Despite the many developments we celebrate as "moderns," it must be said that we are by no means the equals of those who nurtured us. We are their successors only. There is an asymmetry in our relationship with them: while the over/under (parent-child) relationship does not exactly apply as before, the older/younger, predecessor/successor relationship remains—and it deserves to be recognized. We are indebted to our seniors because they enabled us to be and develop in directions not possible without their help. They were what philosopher Sidney E. Hook once referred to as "event-making persons," and we are wise, now and again, to bring this to the attention of the younger generation. Those who nurtured us were "present" to us, open to us, generous in their sharing and steady in their responsiveness. They took our personal needs into strict account and related to us with a teaching, helpful concern. They did not deal with us accidentally or incidentally but on purpose. Our elders deserve the benefit of hearing us repeat truths with which they identify, and those who are younger need the benefit of hearing us report truths that voice values by which all generations find meaning and hope.

Many are the scriptural passages that highlight values for generational togetherness. The Psalms are loaded with such passages, of which Ps. 34:11–14; Ps. 48:12–14; and Ps. 71:17–18 are clearly illustrative. So are many passages from the book of Proverbs. But one should not overlook the import and implications of that grand commandment, "Honor your father and your mother . . ." (Ex. 20:12a). All these scriptures, plus many, many others, are useful for teaching appreciation and advocacy with respect to the elderly; they argue for an emphasis upon communal regard between the generations.

The senior generation struggles not only with the awareness that their time here is shorter than before but also with the debilitations occasioned by aging. They have experienced what T. S. Eliot referred to poetically as "gifts reserved for age / To set a crown upon your lifetime's effort."[3]

William Adams Brown told in his autobiography about Elihu Root, ninety years old, who was asked how it felt to be that age. Root answered: "Things are much the same as they used to be. I can work just as hard as ever I worked—for one hour a day."[4] For many of our elders, much has been taken by life, and whatever remains for them, the sense of loss still seems greater than what is on hand. Our preaching can address this sense of loss.

Biblical realism takes the aging process into strict account. The psalmist's word in Ps. 37:25 is instructive for realism and faith: "I have been young, and now am old, yet I have not seen the righteous forsaken or their children begging bread." Psalm 90:10 is also instructive for realism:

> The days of our life are seventy years,
> or perhaps eighty, if we are strong;
> even then their span is only toil and trouble;
> they are soon gone, and we fly away.

The classic passage describing the process of aging is found in Ecclesiastes 12. It begins with a wisdom warning to the young (v. 1) and then moves into an imaged description of what happens as the body-self undergoes the changes brought on by age (vv. 2–7). The passage is a meditation on those changes, and it accents what remains as most important when "the winter of life" is upon us. I have used this passage now and again as an encouraging word for the elderly; explaining the writer's images helped deepen their appreciation for the attention given in the Bible to the place where life had brought them.

Expositional messages and narratival treatments of relevant biblical texts can help seniors get a faith grip on things. I remember using Ps. 37:25 to this end in a sermon titled "Surprised by Life." In the same vein, I also remember preaching a narrative sermon on Gen. 47:7–10, with the title "Looking beyond Our Laments."[5] Both sermons were prepared and delivered with senior worshipers in mind. The concern was to help seniors reflect on their personal pilgrimage, looking on their lives through eyes of faith.

The elderly who nurtured us need help in handling a diminished pride in being alive. Preaching that nurtures faith and strengthens self-respect can provide such help. A text like Luke 12:6–7, which highlights our personal worth in God's sight, can be used strategically to such an end.

Many among the elderly need courage to keep living. With the circle of long time friends narrowing whenever one of them is diminished by sickness and death, the awareness of being loved is steadily threatened. The question of whom to trust becomes a nagging problem as one has to depend on others who are comparative strangers. Meanwhile, the riddle of time puzzles the mind while aging plagues the body. Two mysteries intersect within us all, aged and young alike—*being* and *time*. Preaching that gives counsel about both is essential, especially for seniors, who are more acutely aware that time is not only something we "take," receiving it as a gift, but something that also takes us—forever onward, and then away, as Isaac Watts voiced it well in that hymn:

> Time, like an ever-rolling stream,
>     Bears all its sons away;
> They fly forgotten, as a dream
>     Dies at the opening day.

Some years ago Howard Thurman shared with me a prayer-poem about the need for courage to live. He did not say if it was his creation or a prized find from someone else's life, but here are its poignant lines:

> Give me the courage to live!
> Really live—not merely exist.
> Live dangerously,
> Scorning risk!
> Live honestly,
> Daring the truth—
> Particularly the truth about myself!
> Live resiliently—

Ever changing, ever growing, ever adapting,
Enduring the pain of change
As though 'twere the travail of birth.
Give me the courage to live,
Give me the strength to be free
And endure the burden of freedom
And the loneliness of those without chains;
Let me not be trapped by success,
Nor by failure, nor pleasure, nor grief,
Nor malice, nor praise, nor remorse!
Give me the courage to go on!
Facing all that waits on the trail—
Going eagerly, joyously on,
And paying my way as I go,
Without anger or fear or regret
Taking what life gives,
Spending myself to the full,
Head high, spirit winged, like a god—
On . . . on . . . till the shadows draw close.
Then even when darkness shuts down,
And I go out alone, as I came,
Naked and blind as I came—
Even then, gracious God, hear my prayer:
Give me the courage to live![6]

Finally, preaching is needed to address the quest of seniors to persist, endure, and be remembered. Strong biblical preaching can encourage the spirit of hope. Isaiah 40:27–31 is an apt text to this end; I have used it to encourage seniors. Psalm 73:24 is yet another such text, and also Ps. 90:17, with its prayer-plea asking God to give a future to the work of one's life.

I must close, and I can think of no better way to do so than to share a report from a noted preacher about an experience that still fires his zeal and preparation for pulpit work. Gardner C. Taylor was that preacher, and he told about the day when he was in the intensive-care room of one of New York's hospitals, standing at the bedside of one of the deacons of his church. The deacon was comatose. The man's daughter stood there beside Pastor Taylor, talking to him about her father's last words to her before he lost consciousness. "She told me of how he spoke in his last rational moments of his love of the church and its time of worship. She said that the last thing he said was, 'I wish I could hear him preach one more time.'"[7] What a tribute to one's pulpit work! Preaching that sustains makes eager hearers want what we are sent to share.

SERMON
# All Things Will Be New

James Earl Massey

*Occasion for sermon:* This sermon was preached on New Year's Sunday in the Park Place Church of God, a congregation whose membership is approximately one-fourth older adults. Park Place is a university church located across the street from Anderson University. When Dr. Massey retired as Dean of the Anderson School of Theology, he was appointed Preacher-in-Residence for the Park Place congregation. The scripture reading for the occasion was Rev. 21:1–5.

> And the one who was seated on the throne said, "See, I am making all things new." Also he said, "Write this, for these words are trustworthy and true."
>
> Rev. 21:5

The ending of each yearly cycle and the beginning of a new year stirs my concern to see the renewal of history itself. This continuing extension of time for life here always stirs my remembrance of the grand visionary themes of the prophets about "the time that shall be." My textual passage holds that theme before us. It was addressed originally to a group of world-weary saints who needed a fresh word of cheer during hard times of harassment and persecution from unbelievers. As he was about to close out his message to those who needed an encouraging word, John did so by giving a verbal glimpse of the future, a descriptive comment about a divine happening that will encompass the whole creation and will shape the contour of human life with details determined and controlled by God alone. The promise he voiced is about history, but history with a distinctly different flavor and focus. Our text encouragingly tells us that the God who has been acting *within* history will one day act fully and finally *upon* life and make all things new.

## I

"I am making all things new." This divine word appeals to an ancient and deep-seated human longing and hope. Martin Luther King Jr. was speaking out of such hope when he said, "Humanity is waiting for something other than blind imitation of the past." And does not that hope bubble anew within us when a new year comes? We long to see history move beyond the problematic past that continues to trouble and plague us. The text therefore makes all the sense in the world, and its message helps us to keep our sense in the world as it is.

The idea, the hope and the longing for renewal, is as old as our human experience of brokenness. The desire to see utter newness is as old as human failure because the human heart has always been stirred by the wish and dream of starting out fresh again. This desire for renewal on our part as humans is reflected in the earliest of human records and it stands grandly detailed in the religions that inform our approach to God and life. All humans, even those who are not stirred as much by religious motivations as we, all agree that this world is amenable to change, and that a difference needs to be made in the human scene to which we are accustomed.

We are conditioned by nature itself to desire changes and to make those changes. Such is the human story. But that story sadly shows a prolonged, blind, and unending imitation of the past. It is the story of limitations, a story of failures, a story of multiplied errors in our attempts to tinker with life and make it qualitatively better. Despite all scientific insights and achievements, the old order stamped in our humanity refuses to yield in full, and we realize with deep pain that we remain trapped in the prison of sameness year after year, decade after decade, plagued by suffering, victimized by sadness, steadily entrenched in personal sin, and longing to see an end to societal madness.

Whither goes our world? How long, O Lord, how long? It is to this question that the divine promise speaks: "See, I am making all things new." The emphasis in the text is upon the pronoun I, and God is saying through the prophet that although life as it is transcends our human control, and that the future for which we hope is beyond our human shaping, God will personally effect the needed changes and will renew all things. The church must find encouragement in this world through its belief about the promised, coming, God-enacted next world. "See, I am making all things new."

## II

"All things made new." Interestingly, this promise does not involve a shift so total that every link with the past will be broken. The promise is about a renewed scene of life for us, a real change in the total state of affairs, but the word John used here for "new," *kainos,* indicates the continuation of something that was, but in an altered form. The emphasis in the promise is that this old world, with its tragic and entrapping history, will undergo some changes to make it so qualitatively different that the conditions under which we now live—a tearful, pained, death-entrapped existence, and the "physical absence" of God—will all be transcended. Thus that incomparably breathtaking statement in verses 3–4:

> And I heard a loud voice from the throne saying, "See, the home of God is among mortals. He will dwell with them as their God;

they will be his peoples, and God himself will be with them; he will wipe every tear from their eyes. Death will be no more; mourning and crying and pain will be no more, for the first things have passed away."

This present earth, with its sin-caused problematic conditions, comprises "the first things," which we know so well. The next world, the new one, will be qualitatively different. That world will have continuity with what we have known here, but it will hold drastic differences because "the first things [will] have passed away."

The promise, then, is about a setting in which all creation will find itself fulfilled. Paul was dealing with this same promise and expectation when he wrote these words to the church at Rome:

I consider that the sufferings of this present time are not worth comparing with the glory about to be revealed to us. For the creation waits with eager longing for the revealing of the children of God; for . . . the creation itself will be set free from its bondage to decay and will obtain the freedom of the glory of the children of God. (Rom. 8:18–19, 21)

Paul was writing about the same promise found in our text.

God has promised to make this happen. God will give us a full life, a substantial and secure life in which pain, death, and human differences will have no place. It will be a life without sorrow, tears, or a feeling of loss. Call the process that brings it what you will: call it renewal, call it renovation, call it transformation, call it the new creation—call it what you will, but the reality of its coming stirs the hope that steadies us while we make our way through this land of "the first things."

Think of it! God is going to give us new heavens and a new earth. This is an encouraging word for those who are painfully involved in history, disturbed about it all, and hungry for the best that our hearts tell us ought to be.

### III

The promise that "*all* things" will be made new should remind us that we have already seen the renewal of *some* things. And that is indeed the case! Yes, aspects of renewal are a present reality. Those among us who have been "born again" know this. We know it in our minds through the truth that renews our will to live as we should. We know it in our spirits, which rejoice in freedom from a previous bondage to the sin habit. We know it in our hearts, where we daily worship God and offer praise with a pleasure known only to those "who have been forgiven much."

Yes, inward renewal is a present reality! We realize this again and again

as our moods, our fears, and our anxieties subside and are altered when we
worship and pray. The active presence of the Spirit of God in our lives per-
forms a renewing service, daily, within the whole self. This is the secret of
the saints, the means for radiant living in the midst of disappointment, loss,
grief, harassment for one's faith, and persecution for one's stand against evil.

James S. Stewart was thinking about the secret of such radiance when
he said,

> I am growing more and more convinced that a great part of the
> secret of achieving steadfastness and serenity in face of the battle
> of life is this—not only to commit your way to God in some high
> moment of conversion, but to do that very thing every morning,
> to go down on your knees and say, "Dear God, I do not ask to see
> the distant scene; but here, for the next twenty-four hours, is my
> life—I give it back to Thee, to guard, to bless, and control."

Stewart then added that this "will give the daily divine miracle its chance
to work out in your experience, and will make all things as new and fresh
and fair as when the morning stars sang together when the world was
young."[1]

The world is no longer young, and we are all aging daily. This new year
will bring another reminding birthday. Decay is at work in all that is
earthly. It is a decay that keeps us seeking help from God as we pray, watch,
work, and live toward that final new order that God has promised to bring.
Meanwhile, we go on serving. We go on building relationships. We go on
being responsible, blessing the lives of others on their way. We go on obey-
ing the mandates of our Master. We go on staying open to God for spiritual renewal. We go on acting not merely out of a sense of stern duty but
out of a gratefulness for grace, knowing that in addition to all that is good
and great so far, the best for us is yet to be!

# IV

When I experienced a call to ministry forty-nine years ago, I became a
working member of a young preachers group in our city. It was a kind of
club, if you will, and during our meetings we ministerial students would
practice our craft before each other. There was nothing casual about our
gatherings; we were in total seriousness as we prepared and preached. I later
learned about other such groups among black churches in cities elsewhere.

A dear preacher-friend who began his ministry at about the same time
as I began, and whose background included membership in one such young
preachers club, recently told me the following story about one of the members of the group in which he first practiced his preaching. The young minister about whom he spoke was a person who suffered daily from muscular

spasms. His head would periodically swing from side to side in uncontrollable jerks, and he walked with a cane because his knees periodically rubbed together. In addition to those problems, the young man was afflicted with poor vision and wore eyeglasses fitted with conspicuously thick lenses. His body was victimized by a genetic flaw and he went through each and every day under great strain upon his mind as well as his body. Yet he stayed in school, attended all the assigned classes, and stuck with the preachers club as they met in session.

In time, that young man's name came up to take his turn to preach to the group. All the other members sat with curiosity, and in sympathy, as he stood before them; of course they were questioning what sort of future he could have in ministry. Secretly wishing that life had not dealt him such a genetic blow, they were wondering how he, pained by his daily routine, would ever manage the rigors of the pulpit service role they all envisioned for themselves.

As that young preacher stood before the group that day, he first asked them to sing a hymn with him. And since they had no hymnbooks at hand, he "lined" for them these words of the hymn on his heart:

> On Jordan's stormy banks I stand,
> And cast a wistful eye
> To Canaan's fair and happy lands,
> Where my possessions lie.

> O'er all these wide extended plains
> Shines one eternal day;
> There God and Son forever reigns,
> And scatters night away.

> No chilling winds nor pois'nous breath
> Can reach that healthful shore;
> Sickness and sorrow, pain and death
> Are felt and feared no more.

> When shall I reach that happy place,
> And be forever blest?
> When shall I see my Father's face,
> And in his bosom rest?

> Filled with delight my raptured soul
> Would here no longer stay;
> Though Jordan's waves around me roll,
> Fearless I'd launch away.

> I am bound for the promised land,
> I am bound for the promised land;

O who will come and go with me?
I am bound for the promised land.
                    —Samuel Stennett

My friend, Samuel D. Proctor, said that after that soul-stirring, vision-sharing song his fellow clubmember did not need to give a sermon. "By the time he finished his song of faith, he had convinced us all that from the worst circumstances, from his pit of agony, it is possible to discover that God is alive, active, aware, and able to sustain us in the total range of human conditions."[2]

Yes, we who belong to the church must find encouragement in this world through gratitude for what God is doing and faith in what God has promised to do. A new birth, by God's touch, puts us in touch with the promised morning of life, and a steady faith and obedience keep us moving toward the fulfillment that is in our future. God has planned it all, and God will fulfill the divine plan in due time. "See, I am making all things new." Don't let anything in this old world make you miss the splendid incursions that are even now breaking through from the new one!

# 8

## Questions That Need Answers:
## An Agenda for Preaching

*William J. Carl, Jr.*

Preaching is more than knowing there are those who need to hear, biblical knowledge, spiritual sensitivity, and pastoral concern; it is also an understanding of the specific needs of those who hear and how to address their needs. In this chapter I will survey some concerns that bedevil older adults—concerns that can readily be addressed from the pulpit.

Preaching to older adults requires a sensitivity for where older adults are, to get into their world of thinking, feeling, and doing. After a brief look at the personal feelings of some older adults, I will address some issues, concerns, and needs older adults experience that are readily adaptable to a pastoral kind of preaching. I will also consider the need for and practice of preaching in a nursing-home setting, and will conclude with a view of the commonality as well as the spirituality of preaching to older adults.

### Feeling What
### Older Adults Feel

Imagine what the ninety-two-year-old widow experienced mentally and emotionally when she left her home of fifty-six years to spend the rest of her life in a crowded rest-home room. In using the lectionary to preach to such older adults it is wise to ask a series of questions such as: What would this scripture say to me if I were an older adult? If I were disabled or infirmed? If I were living alone? If I were deciding how to dispose of my most precious belongings? If I were watching all my friends die? If I were feeling this may be my last Christmas? If I were looking back more than looking forward?

In addition to using lectionary selections, building a file of scriptures that lend themselves to preaching to the needs and opportunities of older adults is helpful. Beyond these general ideas, some specifics need to be considered. Note a portion of a letter written by an older retired minister in response to the question, What should we preach to older adults?

June 28, 1993

Dear Dr. Carl,

I have not forgotten about your request regarding effective preaching to the elderly.

Traumas of magnificent proportions plague the elderly. They rarely seek counsel and are ruggedly independent.

Grandparents and seniors face all the vicissitudes of life experienced by their children, grandchildren, great-grandchildren. They often see the forsaking of family values by the younger generations. AIDS, homosexuality, drug addiction, alcohol, sexual promiscuity, divorce, sexual harassment are not alien to the elderly's world.

Consider the number of women and men who have been sexually abused in their lifetime. If they have not earlier resolved the trauma, it plagues them even to the end of life. Both parents working lead to latch-key children.

The onslaught of Parkinson's, Alzheimer's, strokes, etc. usher the whole family into a totally alien and isolating world.

The brief visits the clergy make in homes, hospitals, etc. do not permit very deep acquaintance with church members' life history. Without this insight how can preaching be effective? To the end of life we need to hear the whole gospel for the whole person!

I hope you will find some of my comments helpful to you. If you would like to respond, I would welcome this.

Yours in Christ,[1]

A review of such concerns and others that follow provides a background for preparing pertinent sermons for older persons as well as all the rest who are on their way to becoming older adults.

## Anger

Even as a positive attitude can contribute to the quality of life, so negative feelings such as anger undermine the quality of life. Older adults, because they are restrained by their increasingly disenfranchised roles in life, often feel anger. Anger is a clear emotional signal that something is unacceptable, that something threatens one's security and peaceful pursuits. Feelings of anger often involve a desire for redress or a vengeful attitude.

Generally speaking, most Christians think anger is an unacceptable emotion and want to deny it or hide it, neither of which is mentally or emotionally healthy, or spiritually or socially helpful. Hence many older adults, who tend to be more circumspect in terms of behavior, sublimate their anger or express it in a passive-aggressive manner.

Preaching on a right understanding and handling of anger is most appropriate, especially when it comes to older adults and their relationship with family members. Sermons that consider the ineffective aspects of being angry with others can be enlightening to those who feel angry. Preaching that includes some guidance on how to calm down, how to redirect one's negative feelings in more positive ways, and how to reflect in a meditative manner on more positive approaches can be helpful.

Jesus had his angry moments (Mark 3:5). Paul said that we should promptly deal with our anger (Eph. 4:25–26). Georgine Lomell Buckwalter suggests that theologically preachers need to redefine the genesis and place of anger. She also suggests some references for possible preaching texts and topics in terms of the understanding and handling of anger, including: the mishandling of anger, 1 Sam. 18:11 and Gen. 4:3–7; the yoked negatives of wrath and anger, Prov. 27:4; the malignancy of anger, Matt. 5:22; the temptation to be angry because of the wrongs of others, Mark 3:1–5; John 2:13–16.[2] Since preaching on the place of anger to those who already have feelings of anger may seem controversial, an inductive rather than a deductive sermon will most likely be more readily received.[3]

## Attitude

As older adults continue to grow older they often feel that living longer demands more than they have to offer. There are times they would like for everything just to stop and let them get off, times when they would like to let the rest of the world go by. Older adults as well as many who are not so old need to glimpse an occasional vignette of hope that validates who they are, that acknowledges that as they grow older they are still a part of what is going on and that the changing scene is the way life is and they can still be a part of it.

Years ago there was a recurring movie short titled *The Passing Parade* that covered events in the passing scene of life, cultural patterns that were fading away, ways of life never to be again. Many older adults remember this movie short and feel that the passing scene of life has already passed them by. John the Baptist said that Jesus must increase while he, John, decreased. Sooner or later everyone who lives long enough comes to that realized stage in life, and it is difficult to handle when it does not occur until late in life. As an older preacher commenting on a younger preacher friend of his said: Socrates had to watch Plato pass him. At this point in life everyone needs help in laying hold of the positive aspects of a negative experience. The issue is how to let go without giving up.

## Autonomy and Control

Everyone needs a sense of meaning, empowerment, and control in life. Some older adults never seem to lose these personal convictions, but many do. G. H. Asquith Jr. points out that C. G. Jung held that the afternoon of life "means the reversal of all the ideals and values that were cherished in the morning."[4] As an older person recalls the pluses and minuses of life, there often occurs an unfulfilled feeling, a diminishing of hope for the future. Add to that the fact that, as the U.S. Department of Health, Education and Welfare reports, "Eighty-six percent of persons over sixty-five have some chronic health problem."[5] Included here are advanced physical illnesses and affective disorders such as depression and paranoia as well as organic conditions of attention, memory, and orientation deficits.[6]

Not everyone experiences the aging process during the later years of life in the same way—some experience more, some less, some seemingly not at all. Whether there actually is a widespread loss of those things that give one a sense of meaning, empowerment, and control in life matters little if the older person perceives a deep sense of loss. What others think or feel about how an older adult should think or feel about the loss of health or the opportunity and ability to do what they took for granted doing before is of little or no consequence—except perhaps in a negative sense. What older adults perceive, however, is most significant and is for them *true* reality. Those who preach to older adults need to take seriously what older adults think and need in the preaching of God's grace as an antidote to correct what is negative and confirm what is positive in the older adult's perceived thoughts and feelings. In addressing an older person's perceptions of the inevitable loss of faculties and functions a preacher should never appear to be patronizing or guilty of stereotypical ageism.

Abraham H. Maslow's work with a hierarchy of needs (physiological, safety, love, esteem, self-actualization) offers thought-provoking insights for preaching.[7] So, too, does Lyman W. Porter's "need satisfaction" questionnaire, based on Maslow's work, which omitted the physiological category and inserted an autonomy category between the esteem and self-actualization needs. Retention of autonomy during the later years of life is a matter of significant concern. That is especially true in light of what Emory L. Cowen, a University of Rochester psychologist, has rightly observed: that psychological wellness involves "having a sense of control over one's fate, a feeling of purpose and belonging, and a basic satisfaction with oneself and one's existence." All of which affects "attitude: mind over matters," as Stanley Jacobson, a clinical psychologist in private practice in Washington, D.C., discusses in a *Modern Maturity* magazine article by that name. Jacobson designates "two components of mental wellness: *auton-*

*omy*—the ability to remain independent—and *control*—the ability to be in charge of one's life."[8]

In addition to problems with the undermining of autonomy and control during the advancing years of life, most older persons prefer a personal touch and don't like being dealt with by remote control, according to John Rother, legislative director for the American Association of Retired Persons.[9] Their only hope, of course, for this kind of treatment may be the church and any pastoral ministry extended to them. The more agencies, businesses, and institutions utilize automated answering systems, the more frustrated older adults become—especially as they have difficulty understanding recorded messages. The government's Social Security Strategic Plan is spelled out in a seventy-three-page document calling for a paper-free future. The linchpin of this proposed high-tech electronic transfer will be the direct deposit of their benefits.

Older adults' lack of direct contact or hands-on control in personal affairs, which sometimes means not even being consulted or given a chance to think for themselves, contributes to an already present sense of disempowerment and in turn defensiveness on their part. Such feelings diminish their desire to be involved in anything, which ultimately robs the church of their experienced know-how, increased free time, and a desire to share their storehouse of monetary resources. All of this calls for responsible preaching about a sense of autonomy, about loss of control, and about others conning older adults into doing things against their will. A good text is Jacob tricking Isaac into blessing him instead of Esau (Gen. 27:1–38).

## Death and Mortality

A sixty-seven-year-old man wrote: "As a boy and youth I developed a sense of invincibility about myself. There was no tree I couldn't climb, no river I couldn't swim, no sport I couldn't be proficient at, and there was never any fear of the consequences of things I tried to do." Then following a water-skiing accident, he observed: "The real significance of that event did not occur to me until years later when I began to reflect on my own mortality." Later, following feelings of depression, he observed, "the thing that really hit me was the sudden realization that life would not go on forever. I didn't know what to make of these thoughts at the time and so I tucked them back in the recesses of my mind to consider at a later time." Finally, facing a second bout of bypass surgery, he concluded: "At some point, and I don't know the exact date, I came to the realization that I am not invincible or immortal and that life is a relatively short sojourn." In the end, he concludes that death is ultimately a part of life that everyone must accept and that such a feeling "comes to us in later years making us more cautious and fearful of the specter, and we become more concerned with using each moment to its fullest."[10] Consider how many older adults have like thoughts and feelings and have "tucked them back in the recesses" of their minds "to consider at a later time." What a fertile opportunity for preaching, not only to older adults but especially to older adults.

The older one becomes, the more one thinks about death. Consider the mother, visiting her son and his family, who looked out toward a peaceful, quiet, shady backyard and said, "I'd just like to be out there under the ground." She wanted to be near loved ones without having to try to keep up with a too-demanding pace of life and the debilitating illness that was soon to take her. From time to time, most older adults need to sense a bit of peace and quiet, a respite from the stress, uncertainties, and anxieties associated with advancing age. Older adults need to hear that it is okay to "lay down the old rugged cross" and embrace the hope of eternity, whether or not that means exchanging their cross "someday for a crown."

Most congregations and church programs are organized around the idea of how to live well, not how to die well, but the how of both is needed. Preaching specifically concerned with the needs of older adults can help to change this prevailing mentality. Birth is generally thought to be a joyously celebrated part of life; death is generally thought to be a dreaded separation from life. In the movie, Forrest Gump's mother rightly observes that death is part of living. The gospel preached to everyone and especially to older adults needs to face honestly that death is a part of life and to affirm the hope of the resurrection and the life everlasting.

Like Job, many older adults live the other side of Easter and need to hear the resurrection hope of eternity proclaimed reassuringly again and again, not just at Easter. They readily identify with Job, who accepted his own mortality and longed for some kind of meaningful hope (14:1–13). As older adults continue to grow older and face more realistically the terminal character of life, it is only natural for them at times to question their eternal welfare, even to doubt their hope for life beyond the grave. Even those who are younger, achieving success and knowing only the now-and-then aches and pains of their younger years, occasionally have doubts—but nothing like older adults do.

The confirmation and reassurance of Christ's resurrection is readily heard by older adults, who realize the terminal character of life more and more every day. Job's longing for something more than this life of hurt and suffering is a reality that most older adults understand all too well and need help in handling. Preaching the gospel to graying temples includes both the frustrated hopes of Job and the exhilarated joy of the early Christians who celebrated the power of the resurrection every Sunday. Glimpses of life after death as seen in an interfacing of Job 14 with John 14 hold all kinds of preaching possibilities.

Preachers who have not worked through their own sense of mortality often fail to grasp the concern of older adulults who daily face the anxiety of death creeping closer and looming larger every day. Older adults are very conscious of three levels of aging—biological, psychological, and sociological—but especially the structural and functional changes in their bodily organs and systems.[11] Even those older adults whose health is good face the ever-lengthening shadow of their own demise as they grow older. Younger preachers tend to think they understand what older folk are feeling about death, but few ever do until they sense that they too may be here today and gone tomorrow. Preachers need to let their people know that they are with them, that they share a common mortality that finds its confident strength in the hope of eternity and the power of the resurrection in Jesus Christ.

All who live long enough go through their own autumnal equinox. At first, there are the enhancing marks of middle age—a few gray hairs, a wrinkle here and there, and perhaps bifocals—and eventually the fading forms of fall that give way to the debilitating winter of life. Preachers need to grasp their own aging process, their own sense of mortality, in order to preach meaningfully to those who are advancing in years and especially those who are terminally ill, with a truncated life expectancy.

## Family

An increasingly important theme that deserves careful attention is that of the family.[12] The traditional family concept of a mother and father with a couple of children needs to be expanded to include the extended family, and that, of course, involves the question of what happens to aging parents when they can no longer care for themselves. There are a host of questions: How do you relate to aging parents? What do you do when a parent's mental processes begin to deteriorate or change for the worse? What about a nursing home and adult day care? How do you handle stressful family relations? Andrew and Judith Lester deal with all these issues and more in their book *Understanding Aging Parents*.[13] Every aspect of this extended family responsibility becomes more complicated as more families depend on two incomes, and the sandwiched-in-between generation feels more pressure.

When older people become dependent, they often develop controlling behavior, using manipulation and especially guilt-inducing tactics. Succumbing to such intimidating behavior is not good for the older person or the caretakers involved. In addition, older dependent persons often get their way by playing one family member off against another.[14] Needless to say, such family relations bring with them a host of issues, questions, alternatives, and frustrations, as well as exhaustion and sometimes family abandonment. In ancient Israel older persons were held in high regard and served as leaders (Num. 11:16). When they could not function that way they were absorbed into the extended family.[15] Such respect and inclusion of older persons for the most part no longer happens.

Preaching, like family therapy, can no longer ignore that the developing stages of one family give rise to the development of another, with each impinging on the other in a gradual, step-by-step phaseout and ultimate demise of the first.[16] Such issues need to be addressed biblically, spiritually, and theologically in light of the best psychological and sociological thought. Such issues are expressed in both the negative and positive aspects of denial and acceptance in both the personal and collective aspects of family systems.

Though an increasing number of sixty-five-year-old and older persons are more active and productive than in the past, the present strains placed on many families by aging family members will increase into the next century. George Barna proposes that by the year 2010 one out of every four senior citizens will have children who are also senior citizens. His 1990 estimate of the number of nursing-home beds necessary to accommodate this exploding older generation was astronomical.[17] It is perhaps not surprising that a small but growing number of older Americans are being abandoned by children who feel overburdened and consider their parents to be either a nuisance or impossible to care for. It is difficult to imagine what it must be like to have one's last vestige of hope dashed when life already seems impossible—to be abandoned by those closest to you, to feel discarded, to be utterly unwanted.

In addressing such a topic preachers need to be careful in the choice of terminology. Terms such as "granny dumping" should be avoided simply out of respect for the feeling of those involved. Every preacher needs to heed the way God judged young boys for being insensitive in tormenting a prophet of God when he was old (2 Kings 2:23–24). Sensitivity is obviously needed in addressing this subject in sermons both to those who are caretakers and those who need the caretaking. It is a matter for informed, responsible preaching, not sometime in the future but right now.

Another aspect of family life today is the increasing rate of divorce and number of stepchildren. Marriage has biblically and traditionally been the accepted relationship of mutual commitment between a man and a woman, legalized by civil law and blessed by God through accepted practices in the church. Various aspects of these time-approved practices are being challenged today. Cecil Murphey addresses some possible texts to consider in preaching on the topic of divorce.[18] Anne W. Simon considers such aspects as the place of stepchildren in a family, becoming a stepchild, being stepchildren and stepparents, and the combination family after remarriage.[19] Most older adults are deeply disturbed by the breakdown of their children's marriages and the resulting care of their grandchildren. Because older persons as parents often tend to feel an undeserved sense of shame and even failure on their part, they are reluctant to express their need for help in handling such trying circumstances. In dealing with such subjects from the pulpit, an inductive or narrative sermon form is the least threatening approach—much to be preferred over a deductive approach.

In an article addressed to marriage and family therapists, John Roland, a professor of psychiatry at the University of Chicago, considers the stressful dynamics and possible approaches to couples when they encounter sickness and/or disability. He considers such key issues as intimacy and communication in togetherness/separateness, psychosocial recovery, cognitive impairment, belief systems, and life cycle.[20] An increasing number of marital partners, who pledged in the prime of life to stay together in sickness and in health, are living long enough to put their pledge to its fullest test. The emotional aspects of intimacy and communication, their togetherness and separateness, the roles of caregiver and care-receiver, together with their psychosocial, cognitive, sexual, and belief systems are being subjected to what is sometimes impossible stress. Preaching to older adults poses a wonderful opportunity to consider such stresses and strains in light of the Christian faith. And preaching on such subjects may well help prepare younger people for such an experience when they too are older.

## Fear

When fear is a rational response to an identifiable danger, a person is provoked to a fight-or-flight response. Some moderate amount of fear is not only acceptable but may be helpful in planning future reactions and inducing a so-called "emotional inoculation," which can help mitigate other fear-induced experiences. Fear-induced anxiety becomes neurotic when it primarily involves one's internal emotions, sometimes with somatic symptoms.[21] Depending on the religious view and practices of those involved, prayer and other worshipful acts can be beneficial. Whatever the case, fear is a reality for those who are truly fearful, and they deserve attention and help.

Jane M. Thibault holds that most people fear the aging process because they believe to age is to:

1. grow closer to death,
2. become physically less attractive,
3. lose physical strength, function, and the sense of well-being,
4. lose social status and power,
5. lose independence,
6. lose the very sense of self,
7. become financially unproductive and a burden to others.

Thibault points out that some "positive aspects of aging, which are not considered to be of special value today, include wisdom, increased ability to adapt and cope with the losses of life, increased freedom of personal time, and fewer social constraints on behavior."[22] Obviously we preachers need to heed the counsel of the old pop song to accentuate the positive, eliminate the negative, and not mess with what's in between. Preaching today seldom speaks reassuringly on the wisdom of the elderly and the ability of older people to cope and adapt, nor does it challenge older adults to use their increased free personal time and their relaxed social restraints to God's glory. A sermon diet of accentuating the positive, eliminating the negative, and not messing with what's in between in terms of older adults is needed and appropriate from time to time.

## Grief

When it comes to preaching to the grieving, we need to distinguish between what Paul meant by "grieving as those who have no hope" and grieving as those who believe in the resurrection power of God in Jesus Christ. Perhaps we need to ask: What is normal grief? How do we help others make the emotional transition from the depths of despair to the heights of hope? How do we help people learn to live with loss and find healing in hope? In preaching the gospel to a graying temple, we're challenged to inspire the faithful fellowship to become a spiritual system for the support of those in their midst who grieve. Sometimes informative preaching that recognizes the reality of death can touch those who grieve with a healing wholeness that God alone can bring.[23]

Funeral sermons and memorial messages ought always to have the older adult in mind.[24] Preaching relative to the resurrection becomes ever more significant for older adults, a message they need to hear proclaimed throughout the year, not merely at funerals, memorials, and Easter services. Death and grief are accepted as realities, but the resurrection and the hope of eternity are even greater realities for people of faith. Older persons as well as others are helped by sermons that proclaim a firm faith in God in light of the alternating experiences of hope and despair.[25] The confirmation and reassurance of Christ's resurrection is readily heard by older adults who are facing their own mortality more and more every day. As the pastor in a large retirement community put it: We celebrate Easter every Sunday.

Preachers often forget that they too are mortal when they are preaching a funeral sermon or memorial message—unaware of the mixed message they are giving, unaware of the incongruity of what they are saying in their sermons and what they are doing in their busy lifestyle—communicating one thing with their preaching and another with their scurrying schedules and cluttered calendars.

## Growth and Development

Luke described Jesus' childhood by saying that he increased in wisdom, stature, and favor with God and others. In other words, Jesus grew and developed intellectually, physically, spiritually, and socially. That process of growth and development is a model for everyone at every stage of life from birth to death. The scriptures are replete with preachable narratives of those who continued to serve God in their advancing years, narratives that can be wed to the stories of many today who do the same. Look at Mother Teresa, Billy Graham (even though his health is failing), and Walter Burghardt, who authored the second chapter of this book and continues to preach and lecture all around the world. And what about those who accept misfortune and continue to make a significant contribution to the lives of others? When Sarah Bernhardt had a leg amputated at the age of seventy, she continued her acting career for another eight years.[26] There is, of course, the growth as well as the service aspect. Pablo Casals was asked: "Mr. Casals, you are ninety-five and the greatest cellist that ever lived. Why do you still practice six hours a day?" Mr. Casals responded, "Because I think I'm making progress."[27] Excerpts from Henry Wadsworth Longfellow's "The Psalm of Life"[28] capture the spirit of the godly soul who would live life to the fullest as long as possible:

> Life is real! Life is earnest!
> And the grave is not its goal;
> Dust thou art, to dust returnest,
> Was not spoken of the soul.
>
> Let us, then, be up and doing,
> With a heart for any fate;
> Still achieving, still pursuing,
> Learn to labor and to wait.

Asked what older adults want or need to hear in preaching, an eighty-five-year-old man readily responded: "Tell them to keep on!" Henry Drummond, in his classic little book *The Changed Life*, confirms this thesis about the ongoing growth process throughout life by quoting Browning: "I say that Man was made to grow, not stop."[29] All humankind—young and old, rich and poor, male and female—need not only to hear how Jesus continued to grow and develop during childhood but to be inspired to emulate Jesus' lifestyle throughout life, even into old age.[30]

## Health

The physical/mental aspects of the human experience may be viewed from a disease/illness, dysfunctional, depressed, declining perspective or from the more positive perspective of a healthy stewardship of life. James A. Hyde surveys biblical views relative to disease and illness in James W. Cox's *Handbook of Themes for Preaching.*[31] Scripture sometimes attributes disease to divine punishment for wrongdoing. Although God forgives wrongs and heals disease (Ps. 103:3), Satan afflicted Job with loathsome "sores from the sole of his foot to the crown of his head" (Job 2:7). Doing what is right in the sight of God was seen as the basis for good health, while doing what is wrong could result in poor health (Ex. 15:25b–26). Even Jesus' disciples believed that some afflictions may be the result of wrongs committed by one's parents (John 9:2). Though some still feel there are data to support this view from both a social and medical perspective, Jesus refuted it from a theological perspective (John 9:1). Both the Gospel according to John and the apostle Paul imply a personal responsibility for health and well-being (John 5:13–14; 1 Cor. 3:16–17).

Healing, of course, is a very significant factor in any consideration of health among older adults. The higher incidence of cancer, heart disease, arthritis, Parkinson's, Alzheimer's, strokes, and other life-threatening and debilitating afflictions for older adults provokes an ambivalence of fear and hope in this age-group. In such illnesses many grasp any possible cure available, whether it be proven or experimental. One older adult wrote, "My most recent heart surgery experience brought personal mortality into sharper focus. I say this because it brought me a previously unfelt awareness of the power of prayer and my own unwillingness to give up life."[32] Likewise, even those who have had little to do with a religious faith in the past pray and seek the prayers and spiritual encouragement of others. What's more, many hope for some kind of miracle. Preaching in this context therefore needs to be well informed in terms of a broad spectrum of health issues, their treatment, and how people respond to them in order to communicate hope in times of no hope. Preachers need to be knowledgeable not only in the most recent thinking concerning these matters but also in terms of the past to distinguish which and what is helpful in preaching to those afflicted.[33] Ministers also need to be acquainted with current factual data as well as their own personal and professional position on questions of medical ethics and some aspects of the law concerning living wills, euthanasia, and other socially sensitive subjects before addressing them from the pulpit.

The stewardship of one's self, health, and well-being offers a positive approach to this subject in terms of the elderly. Jesus told the disciples that the first great commandment is to love God with all one has—heart, soul, mind, and strength (Mark 12:30). In other words, we are created to grow and be healthy—physically, mentally, socially, and spiritually—as Jesus was (Luke 2:52). Since wisdom is with the aged and understanding in length of days (Job 12:12), what better wisdom or understanding is there than the stewardship of one's own mental, physical, spiritual, social health? Even including the physical (which declines more from abuse and disuse than from advancing years), nearly every aspect of one's personal life is capable of improving with active use, even during the advancing years of life. The psychological, sociological, spiritual, and physical aspects of human nature as well as the holistic aspects of health all offer wonderful possibilities for a series of sermons that can speak to all ages and especially to older adults.

## Identity versus Integrity

The value of *being* versus the value of *doing* is a significant issue at every stage in life, but it is an especially important issue for older adults. After all, the ability to do lessens as one gets older, reinforcing one's need to *be* even more than ever before. Obviously there are problems for older adults who have always found their primary worth in what they do. Every adult has a need to establish a sense of self-worth that is not dependent on such externals as financial worth, social status, vocational placement, or professional achievement. It is a basic human need to feel satisfied about one's own life cycle. Older adults need to feel not only that they have something to contribute that they and others feel is important but that they are making that meaningful contribution, whatever it may be. Erik Erikson describes this aspect of life as the "generativity versus self-absorption" stage of development, the seventh of his eight stages of personality development.[34]

To follow Erikson's logic: If an older adult is arrested in a life-cycle crisis (the fifth stage, of identity, for example) he or she will have difficulty in handling an eighth-stage integrity issue. Such a person will lack the congruity to move epigenetically upward and onward in a healthy and holistic sense, since each ongoing developmental stage takes place upon the foundational base of what has already been achieved.[35] Residents in one retirement community often introduce themselves in terms of what their past vocation or profession was. The community's phone book even designates the resident's past vocation or profession. As one resident said: Pity those retirees who give you a calling card from their past work; especially pity those who merely show it to you because it is the last one they have and they can't let go of it. Such persons are doomed to a sense of despair. Most if not all of their identity, which was associated with their former work, is gone, along with their sense of self-worth and reason for being. Their personal and spiritual needs both lie in what Erikson proposes is the final phase of life—the "ego integrity versus despair" stage of human development.

In commenting on the work of noted writers, thinkers, and national leaders, an older church member, speaking as much or more for himself as for anyone else, wrote: "Perhaps it is time for each of us to carry our own burden of expression. Accordingly, I do not want to leave this world without having carried mine, no matter how poorly I may do it, either in substance or in technical terms." Retired and in ill health, he sensed his need not only to *do* as he had done in the past so ably but to *be* as his mature musing at his computer revealed.[36] Preaching to such older adults needs to include remedial ideas vis-à-vis a sense of worth based on being rather than doing.[37]

## Involvement

Since physical, mental, social, and spiritual activities all contribute to personal health even in old age, stewardship of time, talent, and involvement need to be preached again and again. Including examples and stories of role models is appropriate. The pastor of a congregation of thirty-two members near the inner city of a metropolitan center reported that the average age of her congregation was eighty-two. Still they were currently engaged in a multifaceted social ministry to the community, including participation in a prison ministry, an eight-week summer theater workshop for high school students, providing facilities for an adoption center, and providing personal items to inmates in the county jail.[38] This pastor was preaching an active social gospel to older adults at the same time she was ministering to their needs and giving them a purpose in living until they died.

A cancer patient who was treated by others as already counted out of life was asked by her teen-age daughter, "Why don't they let you live at least until you die?" Every preacher is responsible for preaching the word of God so that all, especially older adults have a reason for living until they die.

The preacher's task is to excite the creative ingenuity of the untapped older adult experience, know-how, and need to be needed in and for the ministry and mission of the church. Oren Mead, in his book *The Once and Future Church*, tells about a Lutheran congregation of primarily older adults who were engaged in a ministry of doing laundry for a homeless shelter in a large city.[39] When the bishop's assistant pressed the church to support a fund-raising campaign for a synod camp and conference center, the people sensed little interest or concern on the part of the bishop's assistant for what they were doing in a ministry close at hand. Stewardship sermons need to recognize that the individuality of ministry is broader in scope than merely fund-raising for projects somewhere else, especially in terms of older adults who have the time and need to be personally involved in the ministry and mission of the church.

## Loneliness

In an essay titled "People Have a Need to Come Together . . . ," Robert Weiss suggests that those who speak of being lonely generally feel emotionally isolated.[40] Feelings of emotional isolation often result from a need for someone to depend on and because those who have been left alone often feel inadequate in themselves. Social isolation, however, is different, Weiss says, in that it has to do with having "a place where you have a right to be when you show up." He adds, "Maybe all the people don't like you, but that's not the issue: you have a right to be there." He suggests there are no quick fixes for loneliness, but the most sensible solution is establishing a community of friends.

The question is how to gain the self-confidence to reach out to others or to allow them to reach out to you. Loneliness by its very nature is a terrible thing, and lonely people, like depressed people, are often self-defeating because they believe everything they need is impossible. Those who preach the gospel need to proclaim Christ who was able to help others not only believe in God but believe in themselves, because God first believes in them.

Narrative sermons that relate biblical stories to contemporary stories have contagious possibilities. Consider the grand old gentleman whose eyesight had failed so that he could no longer read, which he had enjoyed doing. His hearing had also failed, but he still loved to visit with others to break up the long daylight hours he spent at home alone. A lifelong Presbyterian, he never expected to be anything else. He, however, told how he had invited two Jehovah's Witnesses who were going door-to-door to come in just because he was so lonely. He told how he had engaged them in a heated discussion, and chuckled and said, "I managed to keep them for two hours."

Many older people confined to their homes are every bit as lonely as this hard-of-hearing, nearly blind eighty-year-old widower, but few are as enterprising in finding temporary solutions to their loneliness. Many older adults experience an almost unbearable sense of isolation. They are in desperate need of meaningful relationships in which they feel loved and accepted. As one elderly person contended: Everybody needs at least five hugs each day. Still, many older people don't know how to form new friendships, find fellowship within a community of believers, or what to do about the emptiness that comes from a nonexistent or marginal spiritual life.

Many who have spent the major part of their lives with a spouse whom they no longer have (because of either death or divorce) need help in understanding and handling their loneliness. The Widowed Persons Service of the Social Outreach and Support Section of the American Association of Retired Persons has published a pamphlet *On Being Alone*. It covers a number of needs and concerns that can be addressed from the perspective of gospel preaching, including such topics as "Bereavement and Beyond," "Permission to Mourn," "When Does Mourning End?" and "Taming Your Fears." It also provides an ample supply of illustrative and quotable material.[41]

In a review of medical findings relative to social isolation and heart disease, the *Harvard Heart Letter* reported the familiar story of an elderly couple who had excellent health for decades, until one of them died. The grief-stricken spouse appeared to be in good condition, yet experienced a fatal heart attack within a year of the spouse's death. Recent investigations, according to the review, reveal a relationship between living alone and increased risk of a fatal heart attack. The relationship of stress and loneliness and that stressful circumstances can be life threatening is indicated by recent investigations which show that "people who live alone have an increased risk of dying after a heart attack." [42]The spiritual and social aspects of loneliness in the context of a Christian community need to be explored for biblical texts that help the lonely, especially in terms of an empty spiritual life. Certainly there are the psalms, the Beatitudes, and some wonderful passages from the Gospels and the epistles that are full of comforting counsel.

## Retirement

When businesses face a drop in profits, they often cut costs by eliminating higher paid older workers, replacing them with lower paid younger workers. Many of these older workers are not ready to be phased out of the work force. Beginning in the 1980s, thousands were pushed into early retirement. Some were given economic incentives, but it was at best a bittersweet experience for most. Few want to retire just because they have to retire.[43] As corporate downsizing continues this pattern, informed preaching on the stewardship of time and talent is needed. Preachers can address this dilemma with the challenging possibilities of being a responsible volunteer. Retirees have more discretionary time than ever before, in spite of the fact that they report being busier than ever before. They are busy because they are determined to do something, and the more meaningful it is, the more they like it and are gratified by it.

Many older adults have a storehouse of know-how and deep down inside would like to feel it is not wasted. In terms of the interplay of the successive stages of Erikson's model of the life cycle, they very likely are wrestling with an epigenetic move from the generativity versus self-absorption stage to the final stage of ego identity versus despair. Most of them have something they would like to pass on so they can still feel they have purpose and meaning. If they are able to share something meaningful to them as well as to others, they will most likely avoid the counterpart of Erikson's integrity stage, which is a sense of depressive despair.[44] Preachers do well to challenge older adults to use this boundless store of time and talent, to channel it into the work of God and helping others, thereby enjoying a continuing sense of personal gratification.

In a newspaper article with the headline "Retirees don't have to be couch potatoes," Billy Graham responded to an inquirer who was finding retirement to be something far from the "golden years" he had expected. The retiree was "bored to death," because all he did was "sit and watch dumb programs on TV." He knew that Graham was "still very busy" and asked, "What is your secret?" Graham responded that "as long as God gives me strength I intend to stay busy. . . . There is far too much to be done for any of us to sit back and ignore the world." Graham then challenged the inquirer to discover God's will for himself and to volunteer his time, know-how, and energy. He concluded by quoting Paul, who wrote to the Galatians, "let us not grow weary in well-doing" (6:9).[45]

People who for a major part of their lives have found their primary identity in their work and then have been stripped of it need help and inspiration in finding a new sense of vocation by responding to the call of God as volunteers in the vineyard of God's kingdom. Some who are homebound and feel incapable of doing anything make the best prayer stewards. Some are good at handling a calling list and certainly in making a telephone prayer chain work.

Sermons on the stewardship of time and talent can appropriately consider the opportunities available to older volunteers and the fellowship aspects of volunteering, as well as the convenience factor of fitting their participation into their own schedule of other activities and the satisfaction gained from such involvement. This type of stewardship sermon needs to recognize that older persons often make better volunteers than their younger counterparts because of their availability, conscientious work ethic, motivation, skills, and experience as well as their dependability and influence and connections with others.[46]

## Stewardship of Wealth

Giving in the later years of life, especially out of accumulated resources, dignifies and makes significant the life one has lived. It is said that those who came of age around the time of World War II will pass on the largest amount of wealth ever accumulated by one generation in U.S. history. They obviously need spiritual guidance in the how of responsible stewardship—not only this side of the grave, but beyond the grave, through wills, bequests, and gift annuities. Jesus devoted a major part of his ministry to preaching a meaningful stewardship of all one has in the here and now as a trust from God. Laying up stores for oneself alone is a matter of spiritual concern both to the church and to those involved as the temples of America continue their graying trend. Here the preacher should consider the Sermon on the Mount (especially Matt. 6:19–21) as well as the parable of the man who continued to build bigger and better barns to store his wealth, to no avail because his soul was to be required that night (Luke 12:16–20).

There's no question, God blesses the prosperity of God's people when they willingly share with others, but not when they hoard at the expense of sharing. The call of Christ is to life and to life lived more abundantly (John 10:10). God's people, even in old age, need to hear that God wants them to be less cautious and more joyous, less prudent and better stewards. Preachers need to tell older adults that God wants them to have the best and not feel guilty about it; at the same time God judges them when they live in their own fine houses and God's house lies in waste (Hag. 1:5), and when they walk away from Christ's call and the needs of others because they have great possessions and are afraid to trust God and let go of them (Matt. 19:22).

An area representative for a major denominational church foundation who was formerly an investment counselor urges preachers to challenge their older church members to catch a vision of stewardship that not only fosters the work of God's kingdom and helps others but can be good for them and their loved ones. Preachers have no business trying to be investment counselors, tax accountants, estate planners, or trust experts, but they do need to know enough to inspire their hearers to be faithful stewards, to help them find a greater joy in feeling less uptight about their own future, and to fulfill their own need to give so they can feel right in God's sight.[47]

## Styles of Communication

Though generic prescriptions are being sought for every brand-name prescription drug, there is no one generic style of communication when it comes to preaching to older adults. Their needs and circumstances change as they move through various aspects of aging—from employment to retirement, from active to inactive, from independence to dependence—and depend on their individual circumstances. In selecting a communication style, preachers need to understand the persons to whom and the circumstances in which they preach, and that is especially true when it comes to older adults.

Preaching to older adults who have not yet retired and to those who have retired but are still living independently is generally the same. Preaching in a retirement center, however, poses some differences. Even though the lifestyle of residents in a retirement center is less involved than that of those who are still in their own home and community setting, they still have many of the same concerns that other adults have: family relations, children, grandchildren, even great-grandchildren, relationships with others (especially nursing-home residents), financial matters, unresolved problems from the past (some dating back as early as childhood), issues of health and grief and death, national and world affairs, and spiritual questions. Their concerns, however, tend to differ in intensity compared with those who are younger due to both the losses and changes that occur with greater frequency during later life.

Beyond the thematic aspects of preaching to older adults in general,[48] there are also specialized aspects.[49] Preaching to the three categories of retirement center persons calls for some differences in approach. A chaplain at a large retirement center in Sun City, Arizona, suggests the following differences in retirement- and nursing-home residents.[50] The independent-living group have their own cottages and are able to attend vesper services. They appreciate substantive sermons that are biblically based and doctrinally sound, or what the apostle Paul called the meat of the gospel, not just the milk of it.[51] Expository, narrative, and even topical sermons that are in touch with current events, problems, and issues are appreciated: the Bible in one hand and the newspaper in the other. The inclusion of humor and stories is desirable, but recycled jokes and illustrations should be avoided. A good understanding and implementation of Buttrick's move system can be useful.[52]

The style of communicating with older adults who are no longer independent and self-sufficient is of necessity different from that which is done with those who live on their own and care for themselves. The communication of the gospel of God's love and forgiveness, of hope when all seems hopeless, of promise when nothing seems promising is even more significant. How to communicate the gifts of faith, hope, and love in a context of dependency is a question. Certainly the subtleties of speech, including puns, paradoxes and hyperbole, are not easily appropriated and therefore inappropriate. Where inductive preaching is a preferred sermon form in many circumstances it is less desirable with older adults who may be experiencing an age-associated decline in rational reflection and inductive reasoning. Whatever the case, sermons are best limited to a brief span of only a few minutes in length. Bible-study-type presentations are often well received and more easily appropriated by those who may be suffering from an increasing attention-span deficit. An expository style with a story line that recalls the familiar and may even evoke the hearer's own story line in an affirming manner works well.

For people in day-care centers, a more devotional approach—meditative, inspirational, and spiritually oriented—is recommended. A free use of the psalms is appropriate because they are comforting and full of hope, such as Psalms 23, 46, 90, 91, 121, and others. Many New Testament passages are helpful in dealing with issues like grief and death, such as John 14; Rom. 8:28–39; Phil. 4:4–8; and 1 Thess. 4:13–18. With day-care center participants a dialogical style of delivery in which the preacher picks up and follows cues from the people themselves is more effective and appreciated. In a health center, lesson-type messages and the use of worshipers' names also helps keep them alert, tuned in, and involved.

In a nursing-care setting, a more casual and personal style of communication is desirable, including a give-and-take dialogical form whenever possible. As much face-to-face contact as can be achieved is helpful for those who are hearing impaired, which incidentally is usually a majority. A surprising number of older adults, however, unknowingly acquire a reasonable ability to read lips, so face-to-face contact is important. Diction is also important, including careful enunciation of consonants. Since consonants carry the meaning and vowels the force of language, a booming voice often tends to confuse rather than clarify conversation. Increased volume, therefore, may sometimes be a hindrance and at other times a help. A slower more deliberate pace rather than a rapid-fire speech pattern is especially appreciated. At all times, the preacher needs not only to be heard but understood with a rhetoric, language, and illustrations that are easily appropriated and in tune with one's hearers.

Preachers need to know not only what and how to preach, but to know themselves as well as those to whom they are preaching in terms of working with older adults and their caregivers. Nursing-home residents need to hear comforting possibilities, not painful calamities. Preachers need to work through their own feelings toward older folk who are slow to change, hesitant to accept new ideas, wed to the familiar, reluctant to relinquish control and full of lethargy, even passive-aggressive. Attitudinal access is a major barrier in communicating with those of limited ability. An honest awareness of one's own attitude toward those who need a comforting word and caring help goes a long way in helpfully addressing the needs of those who are both disabled and dependent or in deciding not to work with them. Here is where an oblique inductive approach in preaching to those who are the caregivers of the elderly can be quite disarming while a head-on deductive approach generally provokes a defensive response.

Unfortunately much programming for the older set in most churches is innocuous, and that is also true for much of the preaching done in nursing homes. Poor preaching, like poor liturgy, is boring and ineffective. Whether in a nursing-care unit or the independent- and assisted-living units of a retirement center or elsewhere, poor communication is the product of a half-hearted effort, the lack of both prayer and a creative imagination. Poor preaching is like a cheap Saturday night special that is easy to come by and that often does harm and seldom if ever any good. Good communication of

God's word demands disciplined study, planned efforts, persistent prayer, and hard work. Good preaching with older adults in mind depends on a knowledge of their past and a vision for their future. That is why the eschatological aspect in preaching to older adults is ever so important.[53]

## A Challenge to Be and to Do

Preaching to those who are older needs to include meaningful challenges to be and do all that is personally possible and realistically gratifying. Inspirational preaching is appropriate at every stage in life, but especially for those who are already in the advanced years of life. Such possibility preaching needs to be broadly inclusive. Not only those who are healthy and able but those who are physically limited and disabled need a purposeful place in society. Ministers need to reflect on their own unconscious attitudes and thoughtless ways of communicating that may create barriers to inclusion for older persons, especially handicapped persons. Several older adult concerns have already been noted in this chapter under the preaching themes of "Growth and Development," "Involvement," and "Retirement." In addition, all those who preach need to use their sanctified imagination in playing with all the sermon possibilities available for encouraging persons of every age-set and especially older adults to discover their own reason for being and purpose for living.

Anything that illustrates a meaningful, ongoing lifestyle in the later years of life offers an indirect way of lacing sermons with helpful hints for older adults. Consider the eighty-three-year-old man who was interviewed on the *Good Morning, America* broadcast on May 20, 1996. He had dropped out of college during the 1930s depression. At long last he had completed his college degree. When asked what he was planning to do, he commented on how many fifty-five-year-old people were becoming unemployed through corporate downsizing. Estimating that these people may have thirty years of possible productivity, he said that he plans to help them see how to begin anew and remain active rather than lose zest for living. He could affirm with the psalmist that these older adults can "still produce fruit", that "they are always green and full of sap, showing that the LORD is upright" (Ps. 92:14–15).

A concern for preaching the gospel to older adults, however, should not give rise to a specialized kind of sermon, lest the worship service end up with a further fragmentation of what has already begun with so-called children's sermons. Yet that's the kind of thing some self-interest groups are lobbying for in so many other aspects. They want others to forget everyone else and take care of them and their kind first and foremost. Imagine what worship could become—a whole catalogue of specialized catering, with children's sermons, older-adult sermons, sermons for teenagers and keenagers, to say nothing about the marrieds and the singles, which could be broken down into major subsets delineated by gender and lifestyle.

If there is to be nothing special, unique, or different about preaching to an older generation, then why consider the how and why of preaching the gospel to a graying temple? Preaching the gospel to older adults does have its unique aspects—but it should not be segregated or sentimental. Concerning worship and older people, Urban T. Holmes writes, "Poor liturgy is *sentimental*"; it is "like a placebo or, even worse, a tranquilizer" that covers up the real ups and downs of life. He says, "It is joy without terror, laughter without tears, and love without fear."[54] Preaching the gospel to the graying temple can and should be not only challenging but exciting, not only informed but inspiring.

J. H. Jowett is said to have related that a skilled attorney told him, "A case is won in the chambers." And Jowett contended that effective preaching is accomplished by what preachers do in their study. Perhaps that is the answer to preaching the gospel to a graying temple: To go back to the drawing board of the minister's study and draft a new plan for how to preach to those who are so often consigned to think "I am who I was." The time has come for preachers to help older adults translate their memories of the past into possibilities for the future in light of God's providential guidance.

Preaching today and tomorrow needs to help older adults be able to joyously sing H. Glen Lanier's wonderful hymn, "For All the Joys of Living":[55]

> We thank thee, Lord, for wisdom,
> Gained from our passing years;
> A storehouse filled with memories,
> The gift of joys and tears;
> For visions that still beckon
> Our footsteps on the way
> Of service that will bless the world:
> Give us new strength, we pray.
>
> Let not the fear of aging
> Consume our future days;
> Give us the daily courage, Lord,
> To serve in untried ways.
> Keep us from weak complaining,
> Of years that now are gone;
> May insights gained each passing year
> Be light to lead us on.*

Just think of being able to help others embrace the wisdom God has granted them through the years for the good of all, to share the visions that will enable them to go on serving in a meaningful way, and to find the strength needful for each day. Just think of preaching in such a way that others live without fear of aging, that they may find courage to serve in untried ways, avoid complaining over what is past, and lay hold of insights from the past that can light the way into whatever the future may hold. That truly is preaching the gospel to and for a graying temple.

**SERMON**

## Graying Gracefully to God's Glory

William J. Carl, Jr.

*Occasion for sermon:* This sermon was written following a conference on aging in the Faith Presbyterian Church of Sun City, Arizona. Faith Presbyterian is a dynamic congregation of primarily older adults with a full-of-life, active program of worship, work, and witness. Even a short visit with these faithful folk is a lesson in how good life can be and that growing old can be fun, definitely a part of God's plan that can be lived out gracefully as well as grace-fully. Even though it is an R-rated sermon (i.e., Retirement-rated), it is not exclusively intended for older adults but—as all preaching should be—it is inclusively intended for people of all ages. The scripture references are Ps. 71:7–18 and Luke 2:25–38.

This sermon is about growing old. I guess I didn't need to tell you—the title gives it away. But before you tune out or tune me out on a basis of whether or not you think you're interested in a sermon about old folk, let me assure you that it's not just about old people, but rather about aging. You say, "So what! That's just a euphemism for being old and as an old song put it, 'Nobody loves you when you're old and gray.'" Ah, but we're all aging. It begins the day we're born and it doesn't end until we die.

We usually don't think of children as aging. We say they're growing and developing. In fact, we call the changes they make growth and development. And that, we think, continues through adolescence and into early adulthood. Then we think we've arrived and along about middle age we'll begin our descent in life. But that's not so, unless we choose to think so and consign ourselves to a self-fulfilling prophecy of declining doom.

As long as we live, we continue to go through a potential growth and development process. That's right, we're constantly in a changing process, no matter how old we are, especially in terms of the four aspects of life. Luke tells us that Jesus increased in wisdom and in stature and in favor with God and others. And that's true for all of us as long as we live if we're willing to take charge of our own growth and development as long as we live. There's no question we can all do something about our physical, psychological, sociological, and spiritual well-being as long as we live. So aging is a lifelong process that affects our well-being every step of the way.

Now you know this sermon is for all of us—whether we're an older adult or on our way to becoming one, hopefully sharing with those who are graying gracefully to God's glory. You don't have to go to Sun City, Arizona—where no one can live that isn't at least fifty-five-plus years old—to see the scene is changing in America. Whether you talk about the local congregation or the hairline of worshipers, the temples of God's people are graying. It isn't a question of whether or not we're all aging and therefore eventually graying, but how do we gray gracefully to God's glory?

The apostle Paul said that whatever we do—whether we live or whether we die—we are to do it all to the glory of God. Jeremy Taylor wrote a magnificent religious classic about *holy living and holy dying.* They go together, you know, especially for all of us who love God and are called to live according to God's purpose. What's more, we're called to do it gracefully. We are a people of grace. We're saved by grace and we're called to live and die by the grace of God. After all, our chief end in life is to know God and enjoy our relationship with God forever. And that's not only for here and now but for then and there, and if we're granted the privilege of growing old, to do so gracefully to God's glory.

Luke tells about Simeon, who was a God-fearing man full of the Holy Spirit. In fact, the Holy Spirit had revealed the coming of Christ to him. And the Holy Spirit inspired him to go to the temple to see Jesus. God had promised that Simeon wouldn't die until he beheld the Messiah. So Simeon went, even though he was old, expecting to see the most exciting thing he'd ever seen and to do the most exciting thing he'd ever done— hold in his own hands the fulfillment of God's promise.

Simeon was doing what we all ought to do: keep on having bigger and better experiences as long as we live. That's what God intends older adulthood to be. As Robert Browning put it, "The last of life, for which the first was made." And that's because, as Browning concludes, "Our times are in His hand." But that's not all. Luke tells how Anna, an eighty-four-year-old widow who'd devoted her life to God, also beheld the Christ child. Both Simeon and Anna were *graying gracefully to God's glory.*

Whoever said that old age has to be dull? Why, often the best spiritual insights we ever have occur when we're older. Abram was seventy-five when he went out to begin a whole new life—just think, a septuagenarian leaving home to begin a new life in a new land. You realize the saying "life begins at forty" is barely half right. Life begins when God calls us to a new beginning.

There's a wonderful Iona Community song that tells how:

> God it was who said to Abraham
> Pack your bags and travel on
> God it was who said to Sarah
> Smile and soon you'll have a son
> Traveling folk and aged mothers
> Wandering when they thought they'd done
> This is how God calls his people
> Loosing all because of one
>
> God it was who said to Moses
> Save my people, part the sea
> God it was who said to Miriam
> Sing and dance to show you're free
> Shepherd saint and tambourinist
> Doing what he knew they could
> This is how God calls his people
> Liberating what they should[1]

So we all have exciting possibilities for growth and development, whatever our age may be. Biblically speaking, advanced years are the blessing of God (Job 12:12). God moves most mightily during our older adulthood, as the biblical record confirms again and again. Look at Zechariah and Elizabeth and the birth of John the Baptist. Remember, God spoke through Isaiah (46:3–4), saying,

> Listen to me, O house of Jacob,
>     all the remnant of the house of Israel,
> who have been borne by me from your birth,
>     carried from the womb;
> even to your old age I am he,
>     even when you turn gray I will carry you.
> I have made, and I will bear;
>     I will carry and will save.

So God is with us all the way. God wants us to keep on growing and developing, witnessing and serving as long as we live.

We've already noted the four aspects of human growth and development, namely the physical, psychological, sociological, and spiritual. Outside of the physical, which declines more from abuse and disuse than from age, all the other aspects of life are capable of improving throughout our advancing years, barring some kind of disease or accident.

The challenge is ours, the call of God is ours—to live to the fullest as long as we live, to witness to our faith, and to gray gracefully to God's glory. H. Glen Lanier's wonderful prayer-hymn puts it so beautifully:

> Let not the fear of aging
> Consume our future days;
> Give us the daily courage, Lord,
> To serve in untried ways.
> Keep us from weak complaining,
> Of years that now are gone;
> May insights gained each passing year
> Be light to lead us on.[2]

Just think of being able to lay hold of the wisdom God grants for the good of all, to find the strength needful for every day, and to share a vision that enables you to live meaningfully. Just think of living without fear of aging, with the courage to serve in untried ways, to quit complaining about the past and lay hold of an insight to light your way into whatever the future may hold. And, as the psalmist put it, to tell all the generations to come about the goodness of God's ways, to proclaim to the highest heavens God's righteous power, to live ever and always *graying gracefully to God's glory.*

# Notes

## Chapter 1

*Chapter Notes:*
*The Graying Temple Is Here and Now*

1. Ross Henry Larson, "Ministry to the Aging by Younger Pastors," *Church Management—The Clergy Journal* 68, no. 9 (August 1992): 18.

2. Younger ministers commenting in 1995 on the discussions of a lectionary group in Arkansas to which they belong recognized this concern and noted the lack of understanding and misappropriation of such significant historical events among their peers in preaching to older adults.

3. *The Presbyterian Panel* of the Presbyterian Church (U.S.A.) in a 1994–1996 Background Report reveals that the median age for Presbyterian church members in 1990 was fifty-four as compared with a 1973 figure of forty-eight. See also the demographic data on the increase of older persons in the United States in "Aging," by C. Z. Benson, in the *Dictionary of Pastoral Care and Counseling*, ed. Rodney J. Hunter (Nashville: Abingdon Press, 1990), 16.

4. Participants in an advanced preaching seminar, spring semester of 1992 at Phillips Theological Seminary, conducted these surveys.

5. J. Gordon Harris, *Biblical Perspectives on Aging: God and the Elderly* (Philadelphia: Fortress Press, 1987), 59.

6. Barbara Nilsen, "A Reflection on God, Suffering and Human Responsibility," *The Living Pulpit* 4, no. 2 (April–June 1995): 8.

7. *Investment Focus: A Monthly Publication for Merrill Lynch Clients*, Merrill Lynch, September 1994, 1.

8. Ibid., 2.

9. Leith Anderson, *A Church for the Twenty-first Century: Bringing Change to Your Church to Meet the Challenges of a Changing Society* (Minneapolis: Bethany House Publishers, 1992), 204.

10. Rodney J. Hunter, ed., *Dictionary of Pastoral Care and Counseling* (Nashville: Abingdon Press, 1990), 808.

11. These comments are based on a personal interview with Rev. Francis Park in 1993.

12. Hunter, *Dictionary of Pastoral Care and Counseling*, 807–8.

13. Edward A. Powers, ed., *Aging Society: A Challenge to Theological Education* (Washington, D.C.: American Association of Retired Persons, 1986), 1.

14. Kenneth Stokes, "A Growing Faith after 60," *Alert* 12, no. 4 (February 1983): 11–13.

15. Joan Rachel Goldberg, "The New Frontier: Marriage and Family Therapy with Aging Families," *AAMFT Family Therapy News* 23, no. 4 (August 1992): 1.

16. William Auld, "Challenges and Opportunities for the Aging," *Presbyterian Outlook* 175, no. 8 (March 1, 1993): 8.

17. Craig Kennet Miller, *Baby Boomer Spirituality: Ten Essential Values of a Generation* (Nashville: Discipleship Resources, 1992), vii.

18. George Barna, "Preaching Does Not Impact Everyone in the Same Way," *Net Results: New Ideas in Church Vitality and Leadership* 14, no. 3 (March 1993): 8.

19. Loren Dutton, *The Vintage Years* (Berkeley, Calif.: Ten Speed Press, 1978).

20. Stokes, "Growing Faith," 11–13.

21. Terry Wallace, "Sensitivity Course Offers Bitter Taste of Aging Reality," *Bartlesville Oklahoma Examiner-Enterprise*, February 25, 1993.

22. E. Leo McMannus, "Euphemisms: Up in Arms over the Subtle Epithet," *NRTA Bulletin* 34, no. 2 (February 1993): 18.

23. Bernice Hunt, "Six Myths about Old Age," *Reader's Digest* 120, no. 722 (June 1982): 113–16. For an additional discussion, see Ken Dychtwald's and Mark Zitter's "The Truth about Elders: Dispelling Five Myths That Can Undermine Your Eldercare Planning," *Healthcare Forum: Leadership Strategies for Healthcare Executives* 30, no. 1 (January–February 1987), and Arthur H. Becker, *Ministry with Older Persons: A Guide for Clergy and Congregations* (Minneapolis: Augsburg Publishing House, 1986), 17–28.

24. Gail Sheehy, "The Pursuit of Passion: Lessons from the World of the Wisewomen," *Modern Maturity* 38, no. 4 (July–August 1995): 43–46, 89.

25. Hunter, *Dictionary of Pastoral Care and Counseling*, 808.

*Sermon Notes:*
*What's So Good about Getting Old?*

1. Arthur H. Becker, *Ministry with Older Persons* (Minneapolis: Augsburg Publishing House, 1986), 36–37.

2. Ibid., 36.

3. Ibid.

4. Ibid., 37.

5. R. Maurice Boyd, *A Lover's Quarrel with the World*, ed. Ian A. Hunter (Philadelphia: Westminster Press, 1988), 146.

6. Ibid., 148.

7. Ibid.

8. Parts of the prayer are from *The Worshipbook* of the Presbyterian Church.

## Chapter 2

*Chapter Notes:*
*Aging: A Long Loving Look at the Real*

1. In recent years the expression "third age" has come to be increasingly accepted. Fordham University's Msgr. Charles Fahey has done much to popularize and deepen the meaning of the expression.

2. In this first section I develop and sharpen a number of ideas published in my article "Aging, Suffering and Dying: A Christian Perspective," *Concilium* (1991/3): 65–71.

3. Simone de Beauvoir, *The Coming of Age* (New York: Putnam, 1973), 322–23. Note how the culture denigrates simply "being" and regards death as an evil that simply happens to us.

4. Here I have been helped by the Opera Pia International volume *Aging: Spiritual Perspectives*, ed. Francis V. Tiso (Lake Worth, Fla.: Sunday Publications, 1982).

5. See Asher Finkel, "Aging: The Jewish Perspective," in ibid., 111.

6. Ibid., 124.

7. Ibid., 130.

8. See ibid., 133. Almost two decades ago Drew Christiansen, "Ethical Implications in Aging," *Encyclopedia of Bioethics*, vol. 1 (1978), 58–65, neatly summarized our ethical dilemmas with respect to the aging: how to maintain a balance between work and leisure, freedom and dependence, economic enterprise and interpersonal life, health care and the acceptance of impairment.

9. Karl Rahner, "Following the Crucified," *Theological Investigations* 18: *Faith and Ministry* (New York: Crossroad, 1983), 160–61.

10. Ibid., 169–70.

11. From my notes of a retreat conducted by Fr. McNamara a quarter century ago in Sedona, Arizona.

12. Here I borrow, with some modifications, material published in my article "Contemplation: A Long Loving Look at the Real," *Church* 5, no. 4 (winter 1989): 14–18.

13. Walter Kerr, *The Decline of Pleasure* (New York: Simon & Schuster, 1962), 210–11.

14. Josef Pieper, *In Tune with the World* (New York: Harcourt, 1965); ancient, if you wish, but not dated.

15. Abraham Heschel, *Between God and Man: An Interpretation of Judaism from the Writings of Abraham J. Heschel* (New York: Harper, 1959), 40.

16. Kerr, *Decline of Pleasure*, 245.

17. Henri J. M. Nouwen and Walter J. Gaffney, *Aging* (Garden City, N.Y.: Doubleday & Co., 1976), 101 and 102.

# Chapter 3

*Chapter Notes:*
*Threescore, Ten, and Trouble*

1. For a study of population shifts along with statistics, see Charles S. Harris, *Fact Book on Aging: A Profile of America's Older Population* (Washington, D.C.: National Council on Aging, 1978–88). See also *A Profile of Older Americans*, (Washington, D.C.: American Association of Retired Persons, 1984).

2. See Juanita M. Kreps, "Human Values, Economic Values, and the Elderly," *Aging, Death, and the Completion of Being*, ed. David D. Van Tassel (Philadelphia: University of Pennsylvania, 1979), 20–26, as cited in J. Gordon Harris, *God and the Elderly: Biblical Perspectives on Aging* (Philadelphia: Fortress Press, 1987).

3. I do not imply that congregations are to provide for the elderly instead of government. During the Reagan presidency there was some attempt to shift governmental responsibility over to charitible institutions and churches. And many congregations bought into the shift. But, properly, societies, through their governmental structures, should provide support for the aging. Perhaps churches must be (1) a prophetic voice calling all of us to responsibility, and (2) a "light of the world," showing an example of tenderness and affectionate concern for the elderly.

4. Israel was actually rather modest in exaggerating ages. By comparison, Sumerian kings are reported to have reigned from 18,600 to 65,000 years. For discussion, see E. A. Spieser, *Genesis* (Garden City, N.Y.: Doubleday & Co., 1964), 41–43.

5. Rachel Zohar Dulin, *A Crown of Glory: A Biblical View of Aging* (New York: Paulist Press, 1988), 18–23; see also Hans Walter Wolff, *Anthropology of the Old Testament* (Philadelphia: Fortress Press, 1974), chap. 13.

6. Dulin, *Crown*, 23–26.

7. Hebrew uses *shevah* ("gray head") as a synonym for general old age, as in Gen. 15:5; Judg. 8:32; 1 Chron. 29:28. White hair, or "wool," seems to be a metaphor reserved for those who are sixty or older.

8. The Hebrew refers to the caperberry. Robert Gordis translates the phrase in Eccl. 12:5 as "And the caperberry can no longer stimulate desire." See discussion of the text in his *Koheleth—The Man and His World: A Study of Ecclesiastes* (New York: Schocken Books, 1968), 345–46.

9. Genesis 15:5 reports the covenant with Abram—"count the stars if you can"—and Gen. 32:13 has Jacob recalling the promise of offspring as many as "sands of the sea."

10. Some years ago I wrote an article that included the following comment: To most churchgoers faith is either "believing what we're supposed to believe"

or is a warm-tub feeling in the heart; either docility or ecstasy! Yet here in Genesis faith is *living* faith, not passive acquiescence or stirred passion. Some years ago a cheerfully indelicate theologian, commenting on Gen. 15:6, wrote a piece wryly titled "Faith as Screwing!" The title may seem indecent, but it is surely apt. Abram bet his life on the word of God, not "cooperating with grace" so much as living his trust in response to God's promise. "The Figure of Abraham," *Interpretation* 42, no. 4 (October 1988): 397.

11. See "The Law Code of Hammurabi," in *Documents from Old Testament Times*, ed. D. Winton Thomas (New York: Harper & Row, 1958), 33.

12. In Israel, a curse (*'arur* = cursed) was believed to have actual destructive power. Is the law referring to a malicious neglect that, in fact, could lead to death as effectively as a "strike"? (See an amplification of the same law in Lev. 20:9.) Certainly stealing from parents is viewed as murderous in Prov. 28:24: "Anyone who robs father or mother and says, 'There's nothing wrong with it,' is the accomplice of a murderer."

13. Note that Isa. 1:2 uses the law in Deuteronomy 21 to accuse Israel: "I reared children and brought them up, but they have rebelled against me." Israel is thus deserving of death.

14. The great paean to respect for the elderly is to be found in the book of Ecclesiasticus, also called "The Wisdom of Ben Sira," written around 200 B.C.E. The passage (3:1–16) begins:

> Children, listen to me, for I am your father;
>     do what I tell you, if you wish to be safe.
> It is the Lord's will that a father should be honored by his
>     children,
> and a mother's rights recognized by her sons.
>
> (3:1–2, NEB)

15. For discussion, see Walter Harrelson's splendid book, *The Ten Commandments and Human Rights* (Philadelphia: Fortress Press, 1980), 92–105. Harrelson devotes separate chapters to the first three commandments, to the fourth and fifth together, and then, finally, to the sixth through the tenth.

16. The phrase "that your days may be long in the land" actually speaks to Israel, an Israel that has been given the "promised land" by God. Thus the commandment is not handing out a carrot-on-a-stick long life to individuals who may be nice to their parents so much as appealing to Israel's social future. For a helpful discussion, see Dulin, *Crown*, 13–17.

17. So argues Willy Rordorf in *Sunday: The History of the Day of Rest and Worship in the Earliest Centuries of the Christian Church* (Philadelphia: Westminster Press, 1968), 9–24, 45–54.

18. See, for example, the discourses in Proverbs beginning "Listen, children . . . "; Prov. 4:1–9; 4:10–19; 4:20–5:23.

19. "Impairment of previously acquired intellectual functions such as

memory and orientation are the most prominent features of senile dementia," according to Coleen Z. Benson. Dr. Benson goes on to discuss Alzheimer's disease as well as slow progressive dementias caused by hypertension, Parkinson's disease, etc.; "Older Persons, Mental Disorders of," *Dictionary of Pastoral Care and Counseling*, ed. Rodney J. Hunter (Nashville: Abingdon Press, 1990), 807–8.

20. Dylan Thomas, "Do Not Go Gentle into That Good Night," *The Poems of Dylan Thomas* (New York: New Directions Publishing, 1952).

21. No wonder that Qoheleth can advise, "Be happy, young person, while you are young, and revel in the days of your prime; follow the impulses of your heart and the desires of your eyes" (Eccl. 11:8). Numbers 15:39b tells us "not to follow the lust of your own heart and your own eyes," but old Qoheleth knows better.

22. We must be cautious: The elderly can fall into a "business as usual" corruption of youthful vision. For example, there is the awful story of the old prophet in 1 Kings 13:1–32. The old man inadvertently misleads a colleague because he cannot believe that the younger prophet has actually had a word from the Lord. How easily the old can become jaded.

23. Gerd Theissen, in *Sociology of Early Palestinian Christianity* (trans. John Bowden [Philadelphia: Fortress Press, 1977]), one of the first attempts to apply sociological analysis to the Christian scriptures, discusses texts that seem to dismiss family ties. In particular, see part 1, pp. 7–30.

24. On the antitheses as a rabbinic form, see David Daube, *The New Testament and Rabbinic Judaism* (London: Athlone Press, 1956), 58.

25. Bernard Brandon Scott, *Hear Then the Parable: A Commentary on the Parables of Jesus* (Minneapolis: Fortress Press, 1989), 99–125; and also his earlier study, "The Prodigal Son: A Structuralist Interpretation," in *Semeia 9: Polyvalent Narration*, ed. John Dominic Crossan (Missoula, Mont: Scholars Press, 1977), 45–73.

26. See my essay, "Preaching about the Family," in *Preaching In and Out of Season*, ed. T. G. Long and N. D. McCarter (Louisville, Ky.: Westminster/John Knox Press, 1990), 28–42.

27. The term *Haustafeln* is from Luther. For a survey of scholarship, see Peter T. O'Brien, *Colossians, Philemon* (Waco, Tex.: Word Books, 1982), 214–20.

28. For a remarkable analysis of economic change during the Reagan era, see Greg J. Duncan, "Economic Poverty—Causes and Effects," in *Standing with the Poor: Theological Reflections on Economic Reality*, ed. Paul P. Parker (Cleveland: Pilgrim Press, 1992), 3–28.

29. See George E. Mendenhall, *The Tenth Generation: The Origins of the Biblical Tradition* (Baltimore: Johns Hopkins University Press, 1973), chap. 7.

30. Translation from Carol L. Meyers and Eric M. Meyers, *Haggai, Zechariah 1—8* (Garden City, N.Y.: Doubleday & Co., 1987), 408–9.

*Sermon Notes:*
*Before the Stars Go Dark*

1. I have struggled to find a better substitute for "vanity." The Hebrew *hebel* means empty breath. Should we use "absurdity" or "nothingness"? Both terms tend to carry with them the penalty of overuse by existentialism. "Vapor" is not bad, but "Vapor of vapors, everything is vapor" is so wide of normal conversational usage as to be impossible. So, because of my own inability to locate a substitute, I fall back on "vanity," even though that word's meaning is no longer what once it was.

2. Some scholars suppose that the clause about God's judgment has been added editorially so as to counter "Follow the impulses of your heart and the desires of your eyes," in view of Num. 15:39b, which tells us "not to follow the lust of your own heart and your own eyes." I agree. The notion of judgment here seems clumsy.

3. Here I follow the suggestion of R.B.Y. Scott (*Proverbs–Ecclesiastes* [Garden City, N.Y.: Doubleday & Co., 1965], 253–54) and substitute *boreka* ("your grave") for *bor'eka* ("your creator").

4. I have added the word "white" to clarify "when the almond tree blossoms"; the phrase is probably a metaphor for white hair. Also I have translated the phrase "the caperberry is useless" as "the aphrodisiacs fail."

5. Ludwig Bemelmans, *Now I Lay Me Down to Sleep* (New York: Viking Press, 1943).

6. Kenneth Fearing, "Confession Overheard in a Subway," *New and Selected Poems* (Bloomington: Indiana University Press, 1956), 99–100.

7. Thornton Wilder, *Our Town* (New York: Coward McCann, 1938), 124.

## Chapter 4

*Chapter Notes:*
*The Biblical Age*

1. For a brief look at a few of the myriad extensive discussions of human development by age, see Sigmund Freud, *Introductory Lectures on Psychoanalysis*, trans. James Strachey (New York: W. W. Norton & Co., 1966 [German original, 1916–1917]); Erik H. Erikson, *Childhood and Society* (New York: W. W. Norton & Co., 1950); James W. Fowler, *Stages of Faith: The Psychology of Human Development and the Quest for Meaning* (San Francisco: Harper & Row, 1981); Carol Gilligan, *In a Different Voice: Psychological Theory and Women's Development* (Cambridge, Mass.: Harvard University Press, 1982); and Gail Sheehy, *New Passages: Mapping Your Life across Time* (New York: Random House, 1995).

2. For some analyses of aging in various historical societies, see David I. Kertzer and Peter Laslett, eds., *Aging in the Past: Demography, Society, and Old*

*Age*, Studies in Demography 7 (Berkeley, Calif.: University of California Press, 1995); and Margaret Pelling and Richard M. Smith, eds., *Life, Death, and the Elderly: Historical Perspectives*, Studies in the Social History of Medicine (London and New York: Routledge, 1991).

3. Peter Laslett, "Necessary Knowledge: Age and Aging in the Societies of the Past," in *Aging in the Past: Demography, Society, and Old Age*, Studies in Demography 7, ed. David I. Kertzer and Peter Laslett (Berkeley, Calif.: University of California Press, 1995), 12.

4. See Robert B. Coote, *Early Israel: A New Horizon* (Minneapolis: Fortress Press, 1990), esp. 9–32.

5. Sue Blundell, *Women in Ancient Greece* (Cambridge, Mass.: Harvard University Press, 1995), refers to estimates that 10 to 20 percent of childbirths ended in the mother's death, while women averaged five to six pregnancies each. This estimate for fifth-century B.C.E. Greek cities probably represents a lower fatality rate than rural Israel five centuries earlier. Cf. J. L. Angel, "Ecology and Population in the Eastern Mediterranean," *World Archaeology* 4 (1972): 88–105.

6. J. C. Russel, "Late Ancient and Medieval Populations," *Transactions of the American Philological Society* 48, no. 3 (1958); Kenneth M. Weiss, "Evolutionary Perspectives on Human Aging," in *Other Ways of Growing Old: Anthropological Perspectives*, ed. Pamela T. Amoss and Stevan Harrell (Stanford, Calif.: Stanford University Press, 1981), 25–58.

7. The variety of the modern world provides interesting parallels. In the urban areas of North America's eastern seaboard, many African American males experience sharply reduced life expectancies as a result of social conditions. Similarly, poor health care increases the risks for many minority women in childbirth, and since the average age for bearing a first child can be in the mid to late teens among many American subpopulations, more than the average number of birth-related deaths occur in these communities. In early Israel, these situations were the norm, and there was no medical technology or nutritional expertise to improve situations radically. However, the sharp inequities in life expectancy between rich and poor Americans would be preventable through a redistribution of social privileges and health resources. For a discussion of ancient Israel's situation, see Carol L. Meyers, *Discovering Eve: Ancient Israelite Women in Context* (Oxford: Oxford University Press, 1988).

8. City life also produced many other social and material changes. For an examination of some changes in gender relations during the early monarchy's urbanization, see Jon L. Berquist, *Reclaiming Her Story: The Witness of Women in the Old Testament* (St. Louis: Chalice Press, 1992).

9. As in our own society, the poorer people tend to work at jobs that require more physical strength throughout life. A job of physical labor often must be kept until retirement, despite changes in the body's resilience. In the ancient world, this probably meant that many people labored until their death.

10. Blundell, *Women in Ancient Greece*, 112.

11. Our society can hardly understand this gulf. In our middle-class culture, with a life expectancy of about 80 years, it would be similar to the presence of a ruling class with 240-year life spans. A president today who was born in the 1750s and who had ruled since well before the Civil War would be beyond the comprehension of the average citizen; the gap of knowledge and experience would create categorical differences in perception. Such a leader might well seem to be magical, if not divine.

12. Note that early Israel formed a society of relatively little innovation, where the benefits of a communal memory (dating back, at most, three decades) far outweighed the advantages brought about by knowing more recent information. Villages were much more likely to face the same problems as in the past than to face new situations. The extent of the modern world's innovation presents a different structure of problems.

13. The changes in diet and lifestyle between village and city would have allowed other differences to arise. For instance, only among the city dwellers might there have been obesity and freedom from being out all day in the sun. These urbanites who might live twice as long, grow twice as large (in weight), and develop a different color and texture of skin would have seemed quite amazing to the villagers, who might have thought of these city folk as almost divine.

14. Interestingly but unsurprisingly, Old Testament traditions concerning places where God will wipe away death (such as in Isaiah 25) are set on mountaintops, in cities.

15. Governmental systems and structures of social privileges that advantage elders, therefore, would necessarily increase the strength and influence of the cities and the urban elite.

16. Note the expectation that God's blessings are visible to the third and even to the fourth generation (Ex. 34:7). This would have been as far as a man could have possibly seen. Does the blessing then indicate a man's prosperity throughout his life, passing down to all those whom he would know, despite the changes within the family?

17. An interesting parallel exists today. In many North American cities, men still control the "best" professional positions, in large part because women did not gain education and experience in a quick progression in their youth. Thus, a fifty-year-old male professional is likely to have many more years of experience than a fifty-year-old female in the same profession, and thus the man is privileged with status and money, due to experience. Similarly, churches have relatively few women as "senior pastors." Our society values years of experience, and this continues to work against many women, even though the reasons today are very different than in ancient Israel, when women died much earlier than men.

18. Several of the Old Testament wisdom texts connect wisdom with the ability to travel and to discern patterns of life elsewhere in the world. Persons

with more years of experience could have traveled more, and thus gained important life experience and connections in other parts of the world, and ancient Israel perceived these things as wisdom.

19. Of course, there were also women among the aged and the wise. Consider 2 Samuel 14, for instance. King David receives strategic, deceptive advice from a wise and elderly woman. She tells a story of her two grown sons; she must be at least thirty herself, and maybe even older.

20. All scripture quotations in this chapter are from the NRSV, unless noted otherwise.

21. Also, the New Testament concentrates almost entirely on the forms of Christianity that grew in the Roman world's cities, and so almost all the Christians found within New Testament texts are urban people, who were likely to live longer than rural people.

22. See also Col. 1:28; 4:12; Heb. 5:14; and James 1:4 for other New Testament developments of the concept of maturity.

23. Of course, the rapid innovation of this society makes youth and adjustability virtues almost as great as experience and age. Constant retraining for all ages seems to be an essential part of appropriate responses to the vicissitudes of modern society.

24. Some recent psychological literature suggests that this may be a pattern in our own culture as well; women become more resilient and open to change with age, while men become more rigid and less willing to try new thoughts and actions as they age.

25. I offer special thanks to Will Carl for his encouragement, and to two friends whose suggestions have strengthened this chapter: Ronald J. Allen, of Christian Theological Seminary, Indianapolis, and Paula M. Cooey, of Trinity University, San Antonio.

# Chapter 6

*Chapter Notes:*
*Venerable Preaching*

Based on the Scott Lecture given at Phillips Graduate Seminary, Tulsa, Oklahoma, March 2, 1993.

1. Since giving this lecture, I have heard a marvelous sermon on this text by Barbara Brown Taylor, in which she suggested that Zechariah's muteness may not have been so much punishment as it was gift, that we all need at times to "be silent before the mystery of God." (Sermon before the Academy of Homiletics, December 2, 1994, Durham, North Carolina.) While she makes a compelling case, I doubt that Zechariah would have perceived what happened to him as gift and believe my point holds.

2. Helen V. Jeter died November 17, 1993. In revising this lecture for pub-

lication, I deemed it better to honor the oral immediacy of the lecture and leave it in the present tense.

3. Jean-Paul Sartre, cited in David G. Troyansky, *Old Age in the Old Regime* (Ithaca, N.Y.: Cornell University Press, 1989), vii.

4. Denise Levertov, *Evening Train* (New York: New Directions Publishing, 1992), 62–63.

5. See Martin E. Marty, "Cultural Antecedents to Contemporary Attitudes about Aging," in *Ministry with the Aging*, ed. William M. Clements (San Francisco: Harper & Row, 1981), 57.

6. So avers Russell E. Mase, in "Preaching and Older Adults," D.Min. thesis, Pittsburgh Theological Seminary, 1989.

7. Jean LaPorte, "The Elderly in the Life and Thought of the Early Church," in Clements, *Ministry*, 44–48.

8. G. R. Owst, *Preaching in Medieval England* (New York: Russell & Russell, 1965), 342.

9. William Shakespeare, *As You Like It*, Act 2, scene 7.

10. Carole Haber, *Beyond Sixty-five: The Dilemma of Old Age in America's Past* (Cambridge: Cambridge University Press, 1983), 10–11.

11. Frederick Hastings, "Mnason, the Aged Cypriote," in *Obscure Characters and Minor Lights of Scripture* (New York: Funk & Wagnalls, 1885), 36, 38, 41.

12. See Paul Pruyser, "Aging: Downward, Upward or Forward?" in *Toward a Theology of Aging*, ed. Seward Hiltner (New York: Human Sciences Press, 1975), 107–11.

13. John A. Broadus, *On the Preparation and Delivery of Sermons* (New York: Harper & Row, 1944), 313–14.

14. Paul B. Maves and J. Lennart Cedarleaf, *Older People and the Church* (New York: Abingdon Press, 1949), 219.

15. Mase, "Preaching," 47.

16. G. H. Asquith Jr., "Pastoral Counseling and Care of Older Persons," in *Dictionary of Pastoral Care and Counseling*, ed. Rodney J. Hunter (Nashville: Abingdon Press, 1990), 808.

17. Urban T. Holmes, "Worship and Aging: Memory and Repentance," in Clements, *Ministry*, 92.

18. Clyde Fant, "Homiletics," in *Aging Society: A Challenge to Theological Education* (Washington, D.C.: American Association of Retired Persons, 1988), 12.

19. See Marc Kaminsky, ed., *The Uses of Reminiscence* (New York: Haworth Press, 1984).

20. Holmes, "Worship," 96.

21. See Walter Brueggemann, *The Message of the Psalms* (Minneapolis: Augsburg, 1984), 104–6.

22. Told to me by Ronald Osborn.

23. Nikos Kazantzakis, *Report to Greco* (New York: Simon & Schuster, 1965), 11.

24. Trevanian, *The Summer of Katya* (New York: Ballantine Books, 1983), 135.

25. See Fant, "Homiletics," 10.

26. Dietrich Ritschl, *Memory and Hope* (New York: Macmillan Co., 1967), 218.

27. It was.

28. Following the lecture, one critic suggested that the story about my mother and Uncle Jack was "hopelessly mired in romanticism." I have certainly been called worse things than a romantic, but I sought to answer in this way: "Each day, when I go to the nursing home, I have to change my mother's diaper with one hand while using the other to ward off her blows. She strikes out at me with fists and curses, until I can finish and hug her into quietness. There is nothing romantic about that and ninety-nine percent of what constitutes my relationship with her now. Call it what you will, but do not begrudge me those magic moments of clarity and grace."

29. Denise Dombkowski Hopkins, "Failing Brain, Faithful God," *Memphis Theological Seminary Journal* 32, no. 3 (fall 1994), 20.

30. This paragraph represents the thought of the author of this chapter and appeared, slightly revised, in Fant, "Homiletics," 11. Lest I be misunderstood, let me add that recent studies reaffirm that older persons, based on their maturity and experience, tend to perform many tasks much better than younger people. See Ronald Schiefer et al., *Culture and Cognition* (Ithaca, N.Y.: Cornell University Press, 1992), 105f. The key is matching tasks with interest and ability.

31. Marcus Tullius Cicero, *On Old Age*, trans. Michael Grant (New York: Penguin Books, 1960), 247.

*Sermon Notes:*
*Clasping Hands across the Years*

1. John F. Kennedy, reported by Theodore H. White in *The Making of the President 1960* (New York: Atheneum Publishers, 1961), 21.

2. See, for example, Margaret Craven, *I Heard the Owl Call My Name* (New York: Dell Publishing Co., 1973), 11.

3. Story shared with a group of ministers at First Christian Church, Whittier, California, about 1982.

4. I owe the theme and much of the material in this and the following paragraph to Halford Luccock, *Unfinished Business* (New York: Harper, 1956), 44–45.

5. Gregory of Nyssa, cited in David F. Wright, "Councils and Creeds,"

*Eerdman's Handbook to the History of Christianity*, ed. Tim Dowley et al. (Grand Rapids: Wm. B. Eerdmans Publishing Co., 1977), 168.

6. James S. Stewart, *A Faith to Proclaim* (New York: Charles Scribner's Sons, 1953), 143.

7. Leroy Garrett, *The Stone-Campbell Movement* ( Joplin, Mo.: College Press, 1981), 667–68.

8. Ibid., 668–69.

9. Paul Zimmerman, "Biblical Peacemaking," *The Disciple* 9, no. 13 ( July 4, 1982): 4.

10. Leslie Weatherhead, *Thinking Aloud in War-time* (New York: Abingdon Press, 1940), 54–55.

11. See William Stringfellow, *An Ethic for Christians and Other Aliens in a Strange Land* (Waco, Tex.: Word, 1973), 137–56.

12. John of Antioch, Chrysostom, "On the Statues: Homily 21," in *The Nicene and Post-Nicene Fathers*, vol. 9, ed. Philip Schaff (New York: Christian Literature Co., 1889), 482.

13. Ibid., 489.

## Chapter 7

*Chapter Notes:*
*Preaching to Sustain Those Who Nurtured Us*

1. See T. Jacobsen, *The Sumerian King List* (Chicago: University of Chicago Press, 1939); Gordon J. Wenham, *Genesis 1—15* (Waco, Tex.: Word Books, 1987), esp. 124–25, 130–34; and T. C. Hartman, "Some Thoughts on the Sumerian King List and Gen. 5 and 11B," *Journal of Biblical Literature* 91 (1972): 25–32.

2. See "Milestones," *Time Magazine*, Sept. 17, 1973, 56.

3. From "Little Gidding," in T. S. Eliot, *The Complete Poems and Plays: 1909–1950* (New York and San Diego: Harcourt, Brace & World, 1952), 141.

4. William Adams Brown, *A Teacher and His Times: A Story of Two Worlds* (New York: Charles Scribner's Sons, 1940), 373.

5. See James Earl Massey, "An African-American Model," in *Hermeneutics for Preaching: Approaches to Contemporary Interpretations of Scripture*, ed. Raymond Bailey (Nashville: Broadman Press, 1992), 135–59.

6. Cited by Howard Thurman in his sermon "What Shall I Do with My Life?" *Christian Century Pulpit*, Sept. 1939, 210–11. Used by permission.

7. See Gardner C. Taylor, *How Shall They Preach*, The Lyman Beecher Lectures, 1976 (Elgin, Ill.: Progressive Baptist Publishing House, 1977), esp. 93–94.

*Sermon Notes:*
*All Things Will Be New*

1. James Stuart Stewart, *The Strong Name* (New York: Charles Scribner's Sons, 1941), 240.
2. See the fuller, written version of this story in Samuel D. Proctor, *"How Shall They Hear?" Effective Preaching for Vital Faith* (Valley Forge, Pa.: Judson Press, 1992), 31–32.

# Chapter 8

*Chapter Notes:*
*Questions That Need Answers*

1. Confidential portions of this letter have been omitted at the request of the correspondent, who also wishes to remain anonymous.
2. James W. Cox, ed., *Handbook of Themes for Preaching* (Louisville, Ky.: Westminster/John Knox Press, 1991), 32–34.
3. Inductive preaching resembles the upper half of an hourglass, in which the various grains of sermonic thought come together in a generally concluded thought that one's hearers may observe for themselves. Deductive preaching resembles the bottom half of the hourglass, with the movement from the preacher's generally concluded thesis to the various aspects of the acceptance and/or application of that conclusion presented to one's hearers. For a detailed discussion of this subject, see Fred B. Craddock, *As One without Authority: Essays on Inductive Preaching* (Enid, Okla.: Phillips University Press, 1971).
4. Rodney J. Hunter, ed., *Dictionary of Pastoral Care and Counseling* (Nashville: Abingdon Press, 1990), 809.
5. Ibid., 16.
6. Ibid., 807–8.
7. Abraham H. Maslow, *Motivation and Personality* (New York: Harper & Row, 1970).
8. Stanley Jacobson, "Attitude: Mind over Matters," *Modern Maturity* 35, no. 6 (December 1992): 37–38.
9. Robert Lewis, "Losing the Personal Touch? SSA Envisions Paperless Future; Enrollees Balk," *NRTA Bulletin* 34, no. 2 (February 1993).
10. The unpublished reflections of Andrew Thomas Leverett.
11. Hunter, *Dictionary of Pastoral Care and Counseling*, 16.
12. Cox, *Handbook of Themes for Preaching*, 109–10; Michael Duduit, *Handbook of Contemporary Preaching* (Nashville: Broadman Press, 1992), 495–98; Clyde Fant et al., *Aging Society: A Challenge to Theological Education* (Washington, D.C.: American Association of Retired Persons, 1988), 9.

13. Andrew D. Lester and Judith L. Lester, *Understanding Aging Parents* (Philadelphia: Westminster Press, 1980).

14. For a discussion of how to deal with such circumstances, see "Tips on Communications" in *Department of Defense Eldercare Handbook* (Washington, D.C.: Office of the Assistant Secretary of Defense for Force Management and Personnel, 1992), 15–16.

15. Hunter, *Dictionary of Pastoral Care and Counseling*, 807.

16. Ibid., 423.

17. George Barna, *The Frog in the Kettle* (Ventura, Calif.: Regal Books, 1990), 203.

18. Cox, *Handbook of Themes for Preaching*, 71–75: e.g., "Marriage—a spiritual union (Matt. 5:31–32; 19:3–9)," "Living the ideal (Mark 10:2–12)."

19. Anne W. Simon, *Stepchild in the Family* (New York: Pocket Books, 1965).

20. John S. Roland, "In Sickness and in Health: The Impact of Illness on Couples' Relationships," *Journal of Marital and Family Therapy* 20, no. 4 (October 1994): 327–48.

21. Hunter, *Dictionary of Pastoral Care and Counseling*, 430.

22. Cox, *Handbook of Themes for Preaching*, 30–31.

23. Ibid., 120–21.

24. See Reginald H. Fuller's discussion "Lectionary for Funerals" in his *Preaching the Lectionary: The Word of God for the Church Today* (Collegeville, Minn.: Liturgical Press, 1984), 593–617.

25. Hunter, *Dictionary of Pastoral Care and Counseling*, 532–34.

26. Jack Canfield and Mark Victor Hansen, *A Second Helping of Chicken Soup for the Soul* (Deerfield Beach, Fla.: Health Communications, 1995), 255.

27. Ibid., 254.

28. James Dalton Morrison, ed., *Masterpieces of Religious Verse* (New York: Harper & Brothers, 1948), 304.

29. Henry Drummond, *The Changed Life* (New York: James Pott & Co., 1891), 5.

30. For a further development of this idea of growth and development during the advancing years of life, see the concluding sermon: "Graying Gracefully to God's Glory."

31. Cox, *Handbook of Themes for Preaching*, 69–71.

32. Andrew Thomas Leverett's unpublished writings.

33. Some older writings in this area include the following: Wade H. Boggs Jr., *Faith Healing and the Christian Faith* (Richmond: John Knox Press, 1956); Morton T. Kelsey, *Healing and Christianity: In Ancient Thought and Modern Times* (New York: Harper & Row, 1973); James C. McGilvay, *The Quest for Health and Wholeness* (Tübingen: German Institute for Medical Missions, 1981); Carl J. Scherzer, *The Church and Healing* (Philadelphia: Westminster Press, 1950).

34. Mollie S. Smart and Russell C. Smart, *Children: Development and Relationships*, 3d ed. (New York: Macmillan Publishing Co., 1977), 635–37.

35. Ibid., 635–39.

36. Andrew Thomas Leverett's unpublished writings.

37. Erik H. Erikson, *Identity: Youth and Crisis* (New York: W. W. Norton & Co., 1968), 135–41.

38. See article titled "Aging Church Finds New Mission: Graying—But 'Not Weary in Well-Doing!'" *The News: Synod of the Sun Edition* 5, no. 6 ( July 1992): 16.

39. Loren B. Mead, *The Once and Future Church: Reinventing the Congregation for a New Mission Frontier* (Washington, D.C.: Alban Institute, 1991), 38.

40. Dennis Wholey, *When the Worst That Can Happen Already Has: Conquering Life's Most Difficult Times* (New York: Hyperion, 1992), 54–61.

41. *On Being Alone* (Washington, D.C.: American Association of Retired Persons, 1987).

42. "The Lonely Heart," *Harvard Heart Letter* 3, no. 4 (December 1992): 1.

43. Robert C. Atchley, *The Social Forces in Later Life: An Introduction to Social Gerontology* (Belmont, Calif.: Wadsworth Publishing Co., 1977), 157.

44. For a discussion of depression during the various stages of the life cycle, see E. James Anthony and Therese Benedek, *Depression and Human Existence* (Boston: Little, Brown & Co., 1975), 337–67.

45. *Kansas City Star*, October 21, 1992.

46. For a fuller discussion of this topic, see the AARP pamphlet *"To Serve, Not to Be Served": A Guide for Older Volunteers* (Washington, D.C.: American Association of Retired Persons, 1986).

47. Cox, *Handbook of Themes for Preaching*, 252–53.

48. For additional information relative to preaching themes and older adults, see ibid., 19–21; Lester and Lester, *Understanding Aging Parents*, 77–109; Samuel D. Proctor, *Preaching about Crises in the Community* (Philadelphia: Westminster Press, 1988), 77–91; Wholey, *When the Worst That Can Happen Already Has*, 3–362.

49. Fant, *Aging Society: A Challenge to Theological Education*, 11.

50. Based on an interview with the Reverend Wilson Yost in 1993.

51. For a thorough discussion of doctrinal preaching, see William J. Carl III, *Preaching Christian Doctrine* (Philadelphia: Fortress Press, 1984), 3–157.

52. David Buttrick, *Homiletic: Moves and Structures* (Philadelphia: Fortress Press, 1987).

53. For a discussion of preaching from eschatological texts, see James W. Cox, ed., *Biblical Preaching: An Expositor's Treasury* (Philadelphia: Westminster Press, 1983), 352–68.

54. Urban T. Holmes, "Worship and Aging: Memory and Repentance," in

*Ministry with the Aging: Designs, Challenges, Foundations*, ed. William M. Clements (San Francisco: Harper & Row, 1981), 91–106.

55. *10 New Hymns on Aging and the Later Years* (Fort Worth, Tex.: Hymn Society of America, 1976), no. 4.

### Sermon Notes:
### Graying Gracefully to God's Glory

1. John Bell and Graham Maule, *Love from Below*, vol. 3 of *Wild Goose Songs* (Chicago: GIA Publications, 1989), 36–38.

2. *10 New Hymns on Aging and the Later Years* (Fort Worth, Tex.: Hymn Society of America, 1976), no. 4.